The Complete Guide to Nudism, Naturism & Nudists

Everything you need to know about nudism. (And why you should try it!)

Liz and James Egger

3rd Edition

Wyeland Publishing

British Library Cataloguing In Publication Data.

A catalogue record for this book is available from the British Library.

ISBN **978-0-9562313-2-1**

First published July 2006 by Exposure Publishing as The Complete Guide to Nudism & Naturism

Second edition published 2009 by Wicked Books

**This edition revised and updated October 2015
Published in the UK by Wyeland Publishing**

www.wyeland.com

Contents

Introduction

What images spring to mind when you think of life in a 'nudist camp'?

The cartoon image of two voluptuous young ladies playing with a beach-ball in some leafy glade perhaps?

A bunch of bearded ageing hippy eco-freaks, eating nuts and hugging trees?

Or a tangle of writhing naked bodies thrashing about in some unspeakable orgy?

Sadly, most non-naturists (known in nudist-speak as textiles), have a completely mistaken view of naturists and naturism, which is hardly surprising given our lopsided view of nudity and the naturist movement's obsessive secrecy and reticence.

Public attitudes to social nudity, in the Western world anyway, range from amused embarrassment, through suspicion, to downright condemnation and hostility. And it's easy to see why. From an early age we are conditioned to believe that the naked body is a shameful thing that should be hidden from view, and that the only reason for getting naked, other than bathing, is to have sex. With the light off, of course.

This is a deeply ingrained idea that lies at the heart of our culture, and it takes a leap of the imagination and no little courage to accept that nudity can be enjoyed as a healthy, innocent and wholesome recreation in its own right.

Happily, increasing numbers of people are discovering just this, and the nudist movement, despite being notoriously difficult to break into, is booming.

It is still a minority affair, however, and many nudists dread being outed for fear of ridicule, rejection, or even persecution. Hence naturism shrouds itself in secrecy and silence to protect its members, the speculation, myths and misconceptions continue, and the vicious circle rolls on.

In the meantime those who are genuinely interested in learning more about naturism are faced with the task of sorting through the rumour and innuendo to get at the truth. Worse still, those tempted to try it may find themselves hacking a path through a thicket of wild and conflicting stories in the hope that the effort is worthwhile.

Because of this, many do not start the journey, whilst others give up in frustration before ever shedding a stitch.

Which is a great shame. Because the destination is certainly worth the difficulties.

So it is for those people who wish to find out more or who are tempted to try naturism for themselves that we have written this guidebook.

We have tried to take the aura of mystery out of naturism and present it in an unsensational and matter-of-fact way.

We give you facts, not wild guesses and imaginings.

We tell you what *really* happens, rather than what *we think* happens.

We explain the benefits and drawbacks.

We give clear, precise instructions on how to become a nudist, what to expect, how to behave, and where to go.

We guide you to a list of resources.

And we let other nudists tell you in their own words about their experience of nudism.

By the end of this book you'll have a real understanding of what genuine naturism is really about. And if what you read tempts you to join us in the wonderful world of naturism, you'll have a clear guide to follow and our book will have served its purpose.

This, in short, is the book we wish we could have read when we first decided to try nudism many years ago.

Using this book

We would hardly be justified in calling this work a *Complete Guide* if we didn't include links and references to additional information that the aspiring nudist may find interesting and useful. For clarity's sake, and to prevent cluttering up the narrative with too much information, the web address of sites mentioned in the text is shown in brackets immediately after the first mention of that site.

Links to more important sites are repeated in the Resources chapter, which also includes links to selected naturist websites, information on books mentioned in the text, and the sources of some of the facts and figures contained in the book.

All set? Then let's get started.

Naturism: An Overview

Nude recreation is becoming increasingly popular almost everywhere worldwide. It has been described as one of the fastest growing leisure pursuits of the new millennium.

And yet it remains something of a paradox. Despite its explosive growth and the huge numbers of people engaged in the nudist lifestyle it remains very much a minority interest. Hundreds of prime-time TV hours have been given over to nudists and their way of life, and yet the nature of nudism remains widely misunderstood. And though many people have been tempted, relatively few have dared to sample the delights of naturism for themselves.

It's time to dispel the myths. So kick off your shoes, take the phone off the hook, get your neighbour to collect the kids, and let's explore the colourful world of international naturism together.

Oh. One last thing. Better turn up the heating. You might not want to put your shoes—or much else—back on again!

What is naturism?

Just what is naturism? Or should it be called nudism? And what's the difference between the two terms anyway?

Let's answer the easy question first.

Nudist and naturist (or nudism and naturism) are two interchangeable words. For most people in the movement there is no difference in meaning, and they will happily use one or the other or both, in the same conversation.

Historically the word *nudist* has been more generally used in the USA, whereas the term *naturist* (or one of its European variants), is favoured in the UK and Europe. Some in the movement insist that there *is* a difference in meaning between the two terms, but most nudists don't get hung up on it.

And neither should you.

So from now on we will use either term at random throughout this book. But let's not get ahead of ourselves.

OK. So what is naturism?

The International Naturist Federation (INF), the umbrella body of the world's nudist associations (but not all naturists, something we'll come to later), defines it thus:

Naturism is a way of life in harmony with nature characterised by the practice of communal nudity, with the intention of encouraging self-respect, respect for others, and for the environment.

Which is sort of OK, but it's a bit of a mouthful and a wee bit woolly for our liking. It doesn't really cut to the marrow. And it's a little out of touch with the real world.

For instance, is naturism really a life in harmony with nature?

Well, we guess it ought to be. A spiritual bonding with the natural world was a fundamental principal of the early nudist philosophy, and no reasonable person today would deny that it is a worthwhile aspiration to work towards.

But this is the twenty-first century, and we have to take a reality check. The truth is that very few of us in the developed world, naturists included, are able to live fully in harmony with nature, however much we'd like to. For much of the year most urban-dwelling nudists have to practice communal nudity in the confines of a steaming, echoing municipal swimming baths that has been hired for the evening rather than a mystic, flower-scented forest glade that has stood since time immemorial, but this doesn't mean that they're not real naturists.

Nor do we need to get communally naked before we can respect other people, the environment or ourselves. Surely this is part of the behavioural remit of every decent person, naked or clothed.

Besides, the nudity doesn't have to be communal before it becomes nudism. An important point, and one which we'll explore later, is that naturism is as much about attitude as it is about companionship. You can be as much a nudist when you sunbathe alone on your lawn as when you share a beach with 3000 other naked people.

Now please, don't misunderstand. We don't mean to disparage the efforts of the good people of the INF, who must have worked long and hard to produce a definition that offended no one and was acceptable to all.

But we feel that it just isn't good enough.

We'd prefer a simpler definition, which is this.

Naturism is the enjoyment of getting as naked as possible, wherever and whenever appropriate, alone or with others, just for its own sake.

By stripping away the well-meaning verbiage that clutters the INF description, we come much closer to defining naturism as it is practiced and understood by most modern nudists, however they choose to exercise their naturism.

Let's look at our definition, and see why we believe it to be more suitable.

We'll work backwards and start with the final clause.

'just for its own sake.'

There are many things that naturists do naked. Mostly they're the same leisure activities that are commonly enjoyed by millions of people the world over. Swimming. Volleyball. Tennis.

Yoga. Walking, talking, relaxing, laughing and socialising. You name it, and naturists have probably done it—in the altogether.

Now it's a fact that all naturist pastimes can be enjoyed clothed or unclothed. One doesn't have to be bare to enjoy them, although some activities such as swimming or sunbathing are actually enhanced by being naked. (Conversely others are definitely better suited to wearing clothes. I'd sit all day in a bath of snakes before I'd contemplate skiing, parachuting or bungee-jumping in the buff, but each of these activities has a small but enthusiastic nudist following.)

But that misses the point. When a naturist decides to do a little naturism, the key idea is to get naked for a while. Everything else, enjoyable and eagerly anticipated though it might be, is really just something to pass the time.

This is the bottom line for naturists. (No pun intended.) We enjoy getting naked *just for its own sake*. Why? Well for many reasons, some of which we'll look at a little later, but until you've tried it for yourself you won't really understand why, so let's accept for now that that nudists enjoy getting naked just for its own sake.

Working on back-to-front through the definition we come to:

'alone or with others'

This could be perhaps the most important point to grasp, as the underlying concept is fundamental in understanding why some people can become nudists whilst others never will.

Remember that we implied just now that naturism was an attitude, a state of mind? Let's explain what we mean.

Most people enjoy being naked for its own sake at some time or other. Perhaps luxuriating in a deep warm herbal bath, maybe relaxing nude in one's bedroom after a cooling shower on a sweltering day or even doing a little skinny sunbathing in a private corner of the garden. (You have, haven't you? It's OK. We won't tell.)

However, convention dictates that these activities should be enjoyed alone, or at best with a loved one. The notion that nude time could be shared with others, especially strangers of the opposite sex, is one which boggles the minds of many otherwise intelligent and reasonable people.

Most of us in the Western world have been conditioned to believe that to display one's nude body to another person— except perhaps a partner—is morally, even emotionally, wrong. Although there is absolutely no logical, physical, historical or spiritual justification for this mind-set, the body-taboo remains a deep-seated part of our cultural make-up.

But there are those who have dared to question this absurd paradigm, and found the courage to break free. It requires an independence of spirit and a massive mind-shift to achieve, but it is the defining benchmark of a real naturist that he or she is at ease being naked, either 'alone or with others'.

Actually that's not quite true. It would be wrong to suggest that genuine naturists are prepared to strip off at any and all times in front of just anybody. Such behaviour belongs to the exhibitionists and publicity seekers who may call themselves nudists but in fact do the nudist movement a disservice.

Because to the true nudist, an important condition is:

' *wherever and wherever appropriate* '

Genuine nudists appreciate that not everyone views nudity in the same light as them. Some people are amused, some frankly bemused, whilst others are absolutely offended by the naked body. Whilst we don't agree with them, we respect their feelings, and accept that whilst we have a right to practice naturism, they have a right *not* to be forced to confront our naked bodies if they don't want to.

why the 'where and when appropriate' is so
nd why many naturist sites are tucked away in deep
woodland or behind high fences. It is not out of fear of being
seen—we are nudists after all—but rather an unwillingness to
offend unsuspecting passers-by.

'Wherever and whenever appropriate' might also apply to
the nudist's own personal circumstances. It might be too cold, or
he or she might feel unwell, or might have an unsightly boil on
the backside. We are nudists, not fanatics, and if being nude
isn't comfortable, or just doesn't appeal for some reason, then
we stay clothed.

Let's carry on with our definition.

'getting as naked as possible'

This is the clause that may need the most explanation.

Having already explained that getting naked is the raison
d'être for naturists, why are we now saying *as naked as
possible?*

This refers back to our previous discussions of attitude and
appropriateness, and can perhaps best be illustrated by a
hypothetical example, which will also pull the complete
definition together.

For our example, let's take three young ladies who we'll call
Millie, Billie and Jilly. (Not being sexist but it's just easier to
illustrate the point using the fairer sex.)

Now in this scenario the three friends decide to take a beach
holiday in Spain.

On arrival at their resort, and not knowing the best places to
sunbathe, they decide to try three different locations over three
days.

On the first day they lounge around the hotel pool. It's very
nice, but because it's a quiet hotel that usually caters for a more

elderly clientèle it's also very staid. Nevertheless, they enjoy themselves. The three girls wear swimming costumes all day.

On the following day, they visit the main resort beach on which, this being a typical Spanish holiday beach, topless (known in the USA as top-free), sunbathing and swimming is almost universal.

Millie enjoys herself but chooses to keep to her one-piece bathing suit. Billie and Jilly remove their bikini-tops and spend the day topless.

On day three, they visit a more secluded beach that happens to be clothing-optional. (Guess you knew that was coming, eh?)

At first they are the only people on the beach, and although Millie remains in her one-piece, Billie and Jilly strip completely to take advantage of the solitude, although Billie is a little nervous at first.

Inevitably, after a little while the beach begins to fill up with more holidaymakers, and although the new arrivals also strip off, Billie gets embarrassed and puts her bikini-pants back on.

Jilly, however, stays nude all day and goes home with a glorious tan and no white bits.

OK. No prizes for guessing the nudist. But we hope you followed the reasoning.

Jilly likes to get naked. She has total body acceptance and likes nothing better than to feel the sun and air on her body.

At the hotel she got herself as naked as possible (a swimsuit). However, because it was not appropriate, she did not strip or go topless.

On the resort beach, whilst Millie preferred her swimsuit, Billy went topless and Jilly got herself as naked as was possible (also topless) and appropriate for the circumstances.

However, on the clothes-optional beach, whilst Billie and Jilly got as naked as possible (nude), only Jilly remained nude when the strangers turned up. It was entirely appropriate (a clothes-optional beach), and she was quite happy to be naked alone or in the presence of others (the nudist attitude).

A simple story we know, but it proves the validity of our definition, which, to recap, is that:

'Naturism is the enjoyment of getting as naked as possible, wherever appropriate, alone or with others, just for its own sake.'

So now you know what it is, let's take a look at who does it.

What sort of people become nudists?

Want to know what sort of people become nudists? Next time you're in a busy restaurant, or walking down a crowded street, take a look around you. What do you see? Men, women and children. Fat and thin. Tall and short, rich and poor, old and young. All sorts, right? And guess what? You're looking at the kind of people who become nudists! Yep, ordinary folks, just like you.

In fact at any nudist gathering you'll find a complete cross-section of society, just as you would at any other gathering of people. Amongst our own circle of nudist acquaintances for example we include a retired test-pilot, a vicar, a ballerina, two army officers, a headmistress and a television actress, as well as numerous builders, housewives, factory workers, butchers, bakers, candlestick makers—you name it. In fact the only thing nudists have in common is that they often have nothing in common except for a shared passion for nudism.

Actually, there *is* a quirk in the demographics of naturism, which is that the overwhelming majority of naturists are white and over the age of 35.

It's perhaps not surprising to discover that young adults are under-represented in the naturist movement—peer pressure, lack of confidence and pressing work and family commitments often leave little time or money for other interests—but the shortage of naturists from other ethnicities is much harder to understand.

It is certainly nothing to do with discrimination; nudists are some of the least prejudiced people on the planet and welcome people of all races, colours and creeds. The actual *reason* for the imbalance between the races is that there are considerably fewer applications to join nudist groups from folks of ethnic minority backgrounds than from white people in the first place, which indicates that the *cause* is likely to be cultural. If this is so, it is difficult to find a remedy. It would be fantastic to see more diversity in the make-up of the nudist population, but ethnic influences are deeply ingrained and not easily swayed, and anyway it would be insufferably arrogant of us to try.

Just as diverse as the naturists themselves are the ways in which they practice their nudism.

Members v Independents

Not too long ago, the only way to get naked in a social situation was to join a nudist club. There were few alternatives unless you wanted to risk prosecution by revealing all on a secluded beach or other remote area, and so virtually all established naturists belonged to a naturist club.

Nowadays things are very different, but despite the changing naturist landscape many folks remain principally club nudists, preferring the camaraderie and familiarity engendered by the club environment to the more independent and free-wheeling but often solitary nudist lifestyle experienced by their more individualistic colleagues.

Although most club nudists also take naturist holidays and use nudist beaches, the club is where they feel most at home. Today there are more than 80 landed clubs in the UK alone, which shows that the concept of club nudism is far from obsolete.

But it's no longer the only way to get naked.

The explosive growth of naturism as a mainstream leisure activity means that the opportunities for social nudity have increased exponentially. (But see the section *It's not all good news* below.) This has led to the emergence of the 'independent' nudist, who shuns the club and nudist federation in favour of a more self-sufficient path. Often rejecting the traditional nudist organisations as being regimented, out of touch, irrelevant and contrary to the original nudist notions of simplicity and freedom, the independent scorns membership of any nudist body and seeks to enjoy nudism on his or her own terms.

And these days it's not difficult. Nudist holidays and cruises rarely require anything in the way of membership or registration apart from the usual details necessary for the booking process. The spread of nude beaches across the world means that anybody who wishes can enjoy free and unrestricted nude recreation at any time without the bother of filling in application forms or paying a fee. And the proliferation of sauna-swim parties, beach groups, internet-based nudist rings and even such esoteric entities as nude dining clubs (really, they do exist), means that you can enjoy a full and active nudist lifestyle without ever going near a traditional nudist club or touching a membership form.

Interestingly, although some independent nudists take pride in never joining any nudist organisation, it is rare for most other naturists to be so elitist. The average nudist will usually mix and match being a club member and an independent, and will utilise all the opportunities to get naked that are available and convenient at that time.

Although a large proportion of the nudist population are not currently members of any club or other organisation, this is usually because the benefits of membership are not perceived to be worth the joining fee rather than because of any real feelings of introversion or noncompliance.

As a result, nudists range from the ardent die-hard who gets naked at every opportunity to the occasional day-stripper who uses a nudist beach once or twice on holiday, and from the stalwart club member to the solitary independent, with every conceivable combination in between. This leads to a wonderful diversity of nudist opportunities, but with so much unregistered activity it is almost impossible to be precise about the number of people who practice nudism.

And to answer the question we posed at the opening of this section *What sort of people become nudists*, the answer is this.

Whatever your shape, age, colour or social status and however you plan to practice your naturism, *you* are just the sort of person who becomes a nudist.

Naturism today

Today, some form of organised naturism can be found in almost every country in the world, with the notable exceptions of most of the Islamic nations and large parts of Latin America, Asia and Africa.

As we've seen, the different ways that people can get naked today means that it's not possible to accurately calculate the actual numbers of people who practise nudism as we define it, but some studies have been done which suggest that the figures are staggering.

For instance, in Europe it has been estimated that over 50 million holidaymakers pay at least one visit each year to a nudist beach during their vacation, and some 15 million regularly enjoy an exclusively nudist vacation.

A Roper Poll commissioned in 2006 found that quarter of all adults in the U.S. has been skinny-dipping or has sunbathed nude in a mixed-gender social setting. Based on current population estimates from the U.S. Census Bureau, the poll suggests that more than 55 million Americans have participated at one time or another in nude recreation. Furthermore, the same poll showed that acceptance of nude recreation is growing, even amongst non-nudists. Three out of four Americans today support nude sunbathing at places accepted for that purpose.

Fifty-four per cent agreed that governments should meet the needs of those who enjoy nude sunbathing by setting aside public land for that purpose and 24 per cent believe that people should be able to be nude in their backyards without interference, even if they may be visible to others.

In the UK a more recent survey carried out by London based market researchers IpsosMori in 2011 on behalf of British Naturism (the UK's national naturist association with more than ten thousand members across over one hundred naturist clubs, swims and other venues) showed a similar trend.

There are nearly four million people who would describe themselves as naturists in the UK, a big increase compared to a similar survey carried out in 2001.

A lower percentage of people have experienced nude sunbathing (10 per cent in 2011 compared to 14 per cent in 2001) and swimming (22 per cent in 2011 compared to 24 per cent in 2001) but a higher percentage have been to a British clothes-optional beach, resort or club (10 per cent in 2011 compared to 7 per cent in 2001). These figures relate to a UK population of about 65 million. I'll let you do the maths.

Let's continue.

One in ten Brits have been to a foreign naturist beach, one in ten has sunbathed nude and one in five has swum nude.

More than 100 British beaches are used by naturists including at least four officially sanctioned naturist beaches.

Eighty two per cent think that naturists are harmless, 5 per cent say that they are sensible. Fewer than one in ten (9 per cent) consider naturists to be disgusting and less than one in one hundred considers nudists to be criminal.

Around the same percentage (1 per cent) would go naked themselves but 5 per cent would be alarmed and keep well away. Only one in a hundred would call the police.

Still with us? OK, maybe we should stop with the figures before your eyes start popping. We just wanted you to know that naturism may still be a minority activity but you'll never be short of someone to talk to.

But it's not all good news

Although it's clear that the number of people who practice some sort of naked or clothes-optional leisure is growing, it's equally obvious that there is increasing resistance to the practice of nudity in public places.

The rise of fundamentalist religious organisations, the political right, political correctness (which in many cases is neither political nor correct) and even some absurd health and safety rulings have all contributed to this assault on nudist activity. In addition, in the UK particularly but maybe elsewhere too, we have lost several fine, long established nude beaches due to public outrage at the activities of the *pretend nudists*, namely the swinger/flasher/exhibitionist contingent who are increasingly using them as the stage for their grisly performances.

Whatever the reason, the general public and the authorities are becoming increasingly hostile to the idea of public nude recreation, and we are being slowly squeezed out of many of our places. Although the opportunities for nude leisure are still numerous and diverse, the actual locations where we can enjoy it are under threat.

Maybe things will change again. Who knows? But until then we should support our nudist organisations who continue to lobby long and hard against oppressive anti-nudist legislation. We should question our politicians and leaders, and remember their response when the time comes to vote. Above all we should act in a responsible, respectable, genuine naturist way. Which, sadly, means that if we should stumble across a nest of pretend nudists playing their deviant games at one of *our* nudist places, we must resist the temptation to throw a bucket of cold water over them.

The Organisation of Naturism

Although the worldwide nudist movement is largely unstructured and unregulated, there is a network of national associations or federations which is the closest thing we have to an 'official' body of world nudism.

These organisations act on behalf of their members to encourage and develop the use of new and existing nudist facilities, provide information to interested parties including the media and newcomers, and to offer general support and advice on nudist matters. Some also publish their own magazine and organise sports events and open days.

It's important to note that membership of these federations is by no means compulsory. Huge numbers of nudists enjoy a full naturist lifestyle without ever joining them, and, as we've seen, some of the more confirmed independents abhor the very idea of organised nudism. In fact in 2013 The American Association for Nude Recreation (AANR - the USA's largest and most long-established organization nudist organisation representing approximately 259 U.S. nudist clubs, resorts and parks) announced that its membership had fallen in recent years from a high of 50,000 to about 35,000, despite a numerical increase in the numbers of people actually enjoying some type of naturist activity. The AANR believes that the drop in numbers reflects the reluctance of younger people to join an organisation which they perceive to be redundant and a little stuffy, preferring instead to practice a more informal type of nudity. If this is indeed the case then the nudist federations have some challenges ahead of them if they are to thrive and stay relevant.

We ourselves are in favour of membership, and we advise all newcomers to the movement to join without hesitation. Apart from anything else, many nudist clubs prefer that you are members of the national nudist association for insurance reasons and may look more favourably on your application to join because of it. But, ultimately, the choice is yours.

Each country where nudism is practised has a national association of sorts, even if it consists of just one correspondent. Some of the best known are:

FFN -Fédération Francaise de Naturisme (France).

NFN – Naturisten Federatie Nederland (The Netherlands).

DFK – Deutscher Verband für Freikörperkultur (otherwise known as FKK – Germany).

AANR – The American Association For Nude Recreation (USA).

BN – British Naturism (UK).

ANF – Australian Naturist Federation (Australia)

The International Naturist Federation

The national federations are in turn affiliated to the *International Naturist Federation* (INF – also known as Federation Naturiste Internationale, or FNI) that has its headquarters in Antwerp, Belgium.

As you'll guess from the name, this is the international umbrella organisation which co-ordinates and facilitates communication between the national federations. It also sets out to inform and guide anyone who has a question about nudism, and organises international meetings between the heads of the federations, the most important being a world congress every two years. It represents the federations of 31 countries, and within these federations there are over 1000 unique clubs, clothing-optional resorts, nude beaches and holiday centres. It also has correspondents in nine other countries where naturism is yet to take off. On the occasion of its 60th anniversary in 2013 INF represented the interests of over 450,000 naturists world-wide and the INF card is the most recognised and accepted nudist membership card in the world.

Membership of the INF is not open to individuals, unless you happen to reside in a country that doesn't yet have an affiliated national nudist federation. In all other cases you become an affiliate member through membership of your own national nudist federation. The most tangible benefit of this is that you will receive an INF ID card, which may be required in order to gain entry to some of the larger naturist holiday centres, although your vacation company can often bypass this requirement.

Whilst it's true that the membership of naturist organisations and federations is on the whole decreasing (whereas conversely the numbers of people enjoying a level of naturist activity is on the increase), they still have an important part to play in the life of the nudist movement. As we have seen, naturism is coming increasingly under attack, and the INF and its associated national associations are the only bodies capable of leading a fight back. But they can't do it without our support.

The Nudist Vacation Industry

While much of the tourism industry has struggled through recession, war and terrorist threats, the nudist niche is thriving. Naked recreation and travel is a USD 440 million-a-year industry worldwide, up from USD 120 million in 1992 according to the American Association for Nude Recreation.

Underlying these statistics is the astonishing fact that growing legions of mainstream holidaymakers are sampling the delights of nudism for the first time, and they bring with them an unwillingness to sacrifice the level of service and comfort that they have become used to.

What has suddenly driven such large numbers of firmly clad holidaymakers to bare all is hard to say, perhaps simply a desire to try something different, but the result has been revolutionary.

Although these holidaymakers may not necessarily identify themselves as nudists, it can be argued that their influence has been behind the astonishing renaissance of nudism in recent years.

Until relatively recently most nudist facilities were, quite frankly, abysmal, and stood little chance of improving. Nudism was an extreme minority interest, and its minuscule support base left it hopelessly under-funded. There just were not enough people spending sufficient money to allow for investment in expensive amenities. The poor facilities discouraged many potential new recruits and the movement failed to grow, which merely compounded the problem. It was a perfect, vicious circle.

And then the holiday industry discovered that there was money to be made out of naturism.

Now the rush of investment means that nudist resorts are often some of the most luxurious vacation destinations in the world, and the trickle-down effect of this upsurge of interest and revenue has resulted in a substantial increase both in the numbers of new naturists and the quality of nudist amenities right across the board.

The vicious circle has, it seems, been broken.

Riding on the crest of the nudist wave is a new breed of entrepreneur—the nudist travel agent. Actually, there have always been dedicated nudist-only travel agents catering to the holiday wishes of the naturist community, but it's a measure of the growing popularity and importance of nude holidays that recently many major holiday companies—including the UK's big three—have started including naturist orientated activities within their brochures.

Nude cruises in particular have become a firm favourite amongst nudist holidaymakers, and one of the main operators in the niche sends many thousands of happy holidaymakers on naked cruises every year, including over 5000 just in the past two years. Its first cruise in 1990 involved 36 passengers on a boat in the Bahamas. Last year it chartered a ship big enough to carry 3000 naked cruisers around the Caribbean and is planning an equally lavish event for 2015. With as many as four cruises a year sailing to the Mediterranean and the Caribbean, the berths are usually sold out within weeks of being announced, with over 70 per cent of reservations coming from previous customers.

Today the nudist holiday is big business. It has at long last become mainstream, and looks set to enjoy continued growth. It is properly organised, professionally managed, well funded and is one of the fastest growing sectors of the leisure industry. As a leading tour operator has remarked, 'Fifteen years ago, the cruise lines wouldn't take my calls. Now they're jockeying for our business.'

Dare we say that things can only – *ahem* – get barer!

A History Of Nudity

Nudity. Our cultural heritage?

In the Beginning, everybody on earth, including your ancestors, were nudists.

For almost the entire span of human evolution our ancestors simply had no use for clothing. For close on a million years they roamed the sweltering plains of Africa as naked as the apes they were so closely related to, unaware even of the concept of clothing.

Biologically modern humans first appeared about 200,000 years ago, but studies of the human body-louse, which requires clothed human hosts to survive, suggest that humans started wearing garments only some 72,000 years ago (plus or minus 42,000 years). This estimate closely matches the archaeological record of the first appearance of clothing-making tools.

Thus for almost two thirds of the time that 'modern' people have walked the earth, clothing was unknown, which implies that the natural condition of the human species is nude.

In fact, it has been estimated (by someone who clearly doesn't get out enough) that over 80 per cent of all the people who have *ever* lived on the planet were nudists all their lives. Except that it wouldn't have occurred to them that that's what they were, because being naked was all they knew.

It's impossible to know how they viewed their world, but it's certain that they saw nudity as a completely natural state. There was no shame attached to the human body. There was no concept of modesty. Naked was just how people were. They didn't even think about it.

But inevitably, over the millennia a swelling population forced a gradual migration northwards into more temperate zones. Perhaps for the first time in history people began to feel cold and looked for ways of protecting themselves against the elements. Climates changed and the need for warmth and protection became even more pressing. Maybe there were other imperatives too, but whatever the reasons change was on the way.

The age of the bearskin leotard had arrived.

The Cover Up

It can't have been very convenient.

For one thing animal skins weren't easy to obtain, and you faced a lethal duel with a snarling 700kg carnivore every time the wife wanted a new dress.

And when we consider that the furs must have stunk fit to wake the dead and been as itchy as sin to wear, we can assume that our venerated ancestors slipped out of them whenever the weather was kind enough to let them.

With the advent of loom technology about 6000 years ago however, things got much better. Cloth could be spun at home and fashioned into some sort of style. Out went the scratchy, smelly animal skins. Clothing became comfortable to wear and safe to obtain.

Gradually cities grew and societies evolved into what we call civilisation. As people organised themselves into large social groupings, clothing took on an additional importance over and above that of merely providing shelter from the elements.

Society became segmented. There were kings and priests, soldiers and slaves, harlots and tradesmen. Clothing could serve as a uniform, a badge of office that helped to indicate your wealth and position in society. Clothing, as well as being comfortable, became convenient.

For the first time since mankind emerged from the primordial swamps a million years before, clothes-wearing became the cultural norm for most of the civilised world. (Of course, those tribes still living in the 'uncivilised' parts of the world knew nothing of all this, and continued to live in a state of blissful nudity for a further six thousand years until the European missionaries came along and introduced them to Christianity, clothes, and civilisation. Not to mention disease, drunkenness and destitution. But we digress.)

Clothing Optional

The move from a state of nakedness to one of clothed-ness was a cultural shift driven by pressing physical and sociological imperatives. It had nothing to do with any moral, religious or even aesthetic objections to nudity as such.

Ancient nudes

Although the people of the ancient world were now mostly clothed, nudity was still commonplace and accepted as part of everyday life. They bathed naked in public. They worked the fields naked when the weather allowed. They exercised naked and afterwards they relaxed naked in the sunshine.

Clothes were merely a convenience, or sometimes an adornment, but never a requirement simply to cover nakedness.

Throughout the ancient Egyptian era, which lasted some 3000 years, ladies— even female members of the royal household—were routinely naked all day in the hottest weather, dressing only in their jewels and make-up for special occasions. Public nudity was especially common for everybody under Pharaoh Akhenaton and his wife Nefertiti (1385-1353 BCE).

The Greeks

To the ancient Greeks the human body was a thing of special beauty. The wonderful statues and other works of art that they've left behind indicate the high esteem in which they held the naked human form, and demonstrate the similarity between their ideas of physical perfection and our own. Everyday nudity was commonplace and it's unlikely that any society before or since has had such a veneration for the nude body.

When the early pioneers of modern nudism looked around for inspiration, the culture of ancient Greece was an obvious choice, and many of the earliest nudist groups were modelled upon the Greek example. Even today many nudists regard the ancient Greek era as a golden age of nudism, and try to emulate, as much as possible, the nudist ideals of that superb civilisation.

The Romans

The Romans conquered Greece, and were in return heavily influenced by the astonishing culture that they'd overrun. Despite their mastery of the arts of warfare and engineering they realised that they were mere peasants when it came to the more refined aspects of civilisation, and they rapidly absorbed and adopted the Greek ideals of beauty. Although never comfortable with the everyday, casual nudity so adored by the Greeks, they were fond of socialising naked in their magnificent bath-houses, and even though the authorities attempted several times to forbid mixed-sex bathing, the populace ignored the law and continued with their naked frolics.

Most other ancient cultures throughout the world shared a love of, or at least a total acceptance of, nudity, and saw no shame in the naked human body.

The fact is that public nudity was commonplace over an unimaginable period of time, and if you had suggested to an ancient Egyptian queen or a neolithic cave dweller that it was immoral, evil or disgusting, they would have rolled about on the floor clutching their sides, convulsed in hoots of derisive laughter.

And then along came the Christian Church, and a veil was—quite literally—drawn over the naked body.

Drawing The Veil

The reason for the early Church's fear and hatred of all things corporeal is mystifying.

As we shall see, neither the Scriptures nor the teachings of Jesus appear to have a problem with simple nudity. Indeed, it seems to have been as accepted in everyday life in the Holy Land as it was everywhere else in the world. For example, baptisms were conducted in the presence of a mixed-sex crowd of onlookers, with both the baptiser and the baptised being naked, and it is apparent that nudity was commonplace amongst the fishermen on the Sea of Galilee—including Peter the Disciple—when we read in John 21:7:

'And so when Simon Peter heard that it was the Lord, he put on some clothes for he was naked.'

According to the Gospel of Thomas -Saying 37, Jesus Himself said:

'When you strip naked without being ashamed, and take your garments and put them under your feet like little children and tread upon them, then [you] will see the child of the living.'

The Church's abhorrence of the naked form is, therefore, all the more puzzling.

Nevertheless, somewhere along the way—possibly from the Gnostics, a religious group who believed that the body was inherently earthly and evil—Christianity picked up a profoundly anti-body bias, and the gentle and tolerant Christian message came to include the warning that flesh, especially female flesh, was sinful. It led to temptation. Temptation led to lust. And of course, lust led to S-E-X, which resulted in unspeakable punishments and banishment from the heavenly realms forever.

As a result, when the Christian Church took over from the Roman Empire as the moral custodian of Western civilisation, the idea that nudity equals sex equals eternal damnation was driven deep into the cultural subconscious. Two thousand years of body loathing, which has influenced the world's attitude to nudity right up to the present day, began.

No wonder we nudists face an uphill struggle!

The intervening period, right up to the start of the twentieth century, was one of unrelenting body-denial, during which an unsophisticated peasantry, believing absolutely the Church's teaching that nudity was a certain route to damnation, kept its clothes resolutely on.

The Georgian fashion for sea-bathing allowed for a brief relaxation of the dress code, and some public nude bathing was common on the beaches of the UK up to the 1840s, but it was a short lived freedom.

The Victorians were perhaps the most rigidly uptight of any people before or since, and their strict sense of propriety dictated that even the legs of

tables should be covered so as not to upset the sensibilities of well-bred ladies!

Clearly, in the face of such absurdities it was time for a change, and in Germany, at the turn of the last century, the seeds of a new movement were being sown.

The New Nudists

There is some uncertainty as to where and by whom these seeds were actually planted.

In 1900 a group of young weekend walkers called the *Wandervögel* (Migratory Birds) became inspired by the work of

German sociologist Heinrich Pudor to hike around the country re-introducing the practice of skinny-dipping wherever they could.

Pudor came to be regarded by some as the father of nudism, and his book *'The Cult of the Nude'*, which promoted the idea that the sun's rays had healing properties when enjoyed in the nude, was hugely influential.

Others point to German philosopher Richard Ungewitter as the true founding father of the movement. In 1905 he produced a series of pamphlets explaining his vision of *Nackt Kultur* (Naked Culture), according to which society should return to a simpler, utopian way of life where clothing would become unnecessary. These publications also enjoyed enormous popularity.

It's probable that both of these figures played an equal part in the birth of the movement. It is, in any case, irrelevant. What is undeniable is that the time for change had come. It was an age that was still emerging from the moral repression of the Victorian era, and to the ordinary working man, poorly housed, overworked and socially underprivileged, nudism was, quite literally, a breath of fresh air.

In 1903 Paul Zimmerman opened *Freilicht Park*—widely accepted as the first modern naturist park—and they flocked there in their thousands.

The modern nudist movement was born.

The years up to the First World War saw a proliferation of these *Nackt Kultur* camps and resorts throughout Germany. In those early days, the focus was very much on a simple, healthy back-to-nature approach. Facilities were Spartan. Alcohol was frowned upon, vegetarianism was *de rigueur* and club activities consisted mostly of exercise, gymnastics and dancing, all performed with a respectful nod in the direction of ancient Greek art and culture.

Unfortunately the Great War brought the explosive growth of the movement to a halt. An entire generation of young men was being annihilated on the killing fields of France and Belgium and there was little enthusiasm or sympathy for nudism amongst a people mourning the slaughter of its fathers, husbands and sons.

At the end of hostilities in 1918 the German economy was in ruins and the post-war government was unable to put the nation back on track to prosperity. It was a bad time for Germany, but the disastrous economic situation proved to be the impetus that turned naturism into a worldwide phenomenon.

Visitors from the rest of Europe and the USA poured into the country to take advantage of the devalued mark and to sample for themselves the nudist resorts of which they'd heard so much. With such an abundance of tourist cash looking for a nudist experience, the resorts, unfettered by government intervention, were quick to reopen their doors and once again proliferated throughout the nation.

It was another time of great expansion and activity, and the movement flourished throughout Germany. Advances in printing and photographic technology meant that it was easier than ever before to produce a mass-market publication, and in 1921 a landmark was reached when 'Gymnos', the first ever nudist magazine, was published.

Over time, many of the camps found it necessary to abandon the pre-war utopian ideals of simplicity and asceticism to appeal to the more hedonistic tastes of the tourists, which resulted in an even greater influx of travellers. These visitors took the nudist message back to their own countries, thereby hastening the spread of the modern nudist movement around the globe. For the second time in history, nudism was about to go worldwide!

It's a Nude World

But it wasn't going to be all plain sailing, and ironically it is within the land of the free that nudism has had to struggle hardest to take root.

The American Social Nudism movement was founded by German expatriate Kurt Barthel on Labor Day 1929, and by December of that year it had grown to include some 50 members, at which time it was decided to change the name to the American League for Physical Culture (ALPC).

The growth of the movement was given a boost in 1931 by the publication of the influential book *'Among the Nudists'* by Frances and Mason Merrill, which brought the ALPC and nudism to the attention of millions of ordinary Americans for the first time and encouraged them to try it for themselves. Mainly as a result of the book the ALPC's membership doubled, and thousands went on to form their own clubs.

Despite the encouraging start and the impetus provided by the book however, the combined effects of the depression, war, and the religious right took its toll. The nudist movement slowly went into a decline, typified by the enforcement of the Comstock Act which declared nudist magazines obscene. The 40s and 50s were difficult decades for naturism in the USA. The movement was at its lowest ebb, and the future looked bleak.

And then the sixties happened. Attitudes changed. Suddenly it was 'right on' to challenge the accepted order and experiment with new ideas. Nudism became cool again, and TV screens displayed images of young men and women gleefully disporting themselves naked at Woodstock. Although the older generation may not have fully approved, nudism was at least back out in the open.

Unfortunately though, the sexual revolution proved to be a mixed blessing.

In 1958 The US Supreme Court decided that nudist magazines were not obscene, and a sprinkling of so called 'nudist' magazines began to appear on the news-stands. This trickle turned into a full-scale deluge as the sixties really started to swing, and the market was flooded by semi-pornographic publications calling themselves nudist magazines. Almost inevitably the nudist movement, whilst benefiting from the new openness ushered in by the sixties revolution, found itself confused with and linked to the sex industry. (A similar situation exists today, with thousands of porn websites calling themselves naturist sites, leaving the public with a very confused idea as to what genuine naturism really is.)

Today, naturism is well established across the USA, and although progress is slow and opposition is fierce—and growing —there are encouraging signs that social nudity is gradually becoming increasingly acceptable to most Americans.

However, there is within the American psyche an undercurrent of prudishness that prevents the ready acceptance of nude culture. Toplessness (top-freedom) is still not allowed in public places and there are few public clothes-optional beaches. Whilst graphic depictions of death and violence are commonplace on American television, the nation goes into a collective decline if a bare breast is shown on mainstream channels.

It seems the USA still has some way to go, compared to Europe.

There, things are *very* different.

Vive le difference!

American visitors are often amazed at the degree to which social nudity and body freedom are practiced in Europe.

Top-freedom is almost universal and many of the most popular public beaches, sections of urban parks, spas and resorts are clothing-optional. Full-frontal nudity is common on European television and in magazines.

Social nudity has swiftly become an integral part of the burgeoning leisure scene. The nudist movement, driven by the growth of the mass holiday industry, has moved away from the original idea of bonding with nature and become much more of a mainstream recreational and leisure activity.

Now nudist resorts flourish throughout Europe and one of the largest holiday centres in the world, France's Cap d'Agde, has an all-nude section with a population of over 40,000 nudists at the height of the season.

Today, an estimated 15 million Europeans regularly enjoy naturist holidays and nudism is one of the fastest growing sectors of the leisure industry. In Europe, at least, we are getting back to our roots.

Our ancestors would have been proud.

12 Reasons To Become A Nudist

We are indebted to Mr K Bacher, on whose seminal work '205 Arguments for Naturism' much of this section is based. Mr Bacher's study is enormously scholarly, and fully supported by references and footnotes.

If you are interested in reading this unique reference work in full you can find it in handy downloadable e-book form at our naturist blog at *http://snipurl.com/bacher2*

So far we've examined the historical evolution of nudism and taken a look at the state of naturism today. Now it's time to get down to basics and ask the fundamental question.

Why would anyone want to try naturism?

Because, let's be honest, compared to most other pastimes, getting naked for pleasure is a pretty weird thing to do. It defies conventional thinking. It appears to be illogical. So why on earth do apparently sane people do it? What possible motive can intelligent folk like us have for getting together with a bunch of people we barely know and stripping off just for the sake of it?

To be different perhaps? To cock-a-snook at convention? Because we're a bit strange? Or is there a darker, more perverse reason?

Well of course the simple answer is *why not?* and in a way that just about sums it up. Lots of people take up illogical pastimes just because they want to and they can. Mountain climbing, smoking or drinking alcohol are all activities that don't make a lot of sense to the uninitiated and require a dogged persistence and considerable expenditure before any sort of proficiency or pleasure is obtained, yet thousands of people worldwide do these things on a daily basis. They work at it, overcoming the initial difficulties, because they want to.

Naturists are no different, except that nudism, unlike these other activities, won't damage your health. Quite the opposite in fact.

But you wouldn't thank us for leaving it at that, and anyway there are many other genuine reasons to take up nudism, some of which we're about to share with you.

Firstly though, you must promise to keep an open mind.

If you find the concept of social nudity objectionable or just plain silly and have picked up this book merely for its snigger value, then this section in particular will be a complete waste of your time. No list of benefits, however long or persuasively presented, will change your mind. By all means enjoy the rest of the book. We'll tell you the truth about naturism. But we can't alter a fixed attitude.

If, on the other hand, you've already made up your mind that you are going to become a nudist no matter what, then this section is largely superfluous, although we recommend that you read it anyway. If you are ever challenged to give one good reason why perfectly normal people make a habit out of taking off their clothes (and at some time you will), you'll find plenty of juicy ones here.

This section will be of most value to those of you who find something intriguing about nudism but have yet to fully see the light. If you are sympathetic to the idea of naturism but see no reason to join the nudist family yourself, watch out. This section may change your life.

We have to confess that we've also written this chapter for ourselves, because it's always nice to have some good reasons for doing something that one likes.

31

Nudism is a uniquely holistic activity inasmuch as it satisfies the needs of the body, mind and soul. Consequently therefore, the benefits fall neatly into three groups; physical, mental and social, and that's the way they're presented here. There are, no doubt, a multitude of other reasons why you should become a nudist, and any experienced nudists who read this book will be able to point out many not listed here. But space is limited, and twelve is Liz's lucky number, so we've restricted ourselves to a nice round dozen.

Besides, the real joy lies in discovering the remainder for yourself.

The Physical Benefits

Reason 1:Evidence seems to indicate that there is no physical need for clothing, even in the most extreme conditions!

Although it is generally believed that humans donned animal skins in order to combat the colder temperatures experienced as mankind migrated northwards, there are alternative theories.

One highly plausible hypothesis contends that clothing developed from the basic instinct of human beings to ornament themselves, possibly to enhance sexual attraction.

Yet another claims that shamanism and ritual were the drivers, as the early hunters dressed themselves in the skins of the animals they hunted in order to 'become' them, thus ensuring their co-operation in the hunt.

Whichever theory we subscribe to, the plain truth is that there is no evidence that clothing is necessary for human survival, even in quite cruel environments. In fact the opposite seems to be true.

Tierra del Fuego, which is situated at the southernmost tip of South America, has an extremely hostile climate. The average annual temperature is about 6°C (about 43°F), and precipitation is about 635mm (about 25in). On the mountain slopes facing the wind, rain is almost continuous. And yet, up to and after the land was visited by Charles Darwin in 1832 the native Indians lived completely naked, even in the harshest weather. Darwin himself was particularly struck by the sight of snow melting on the naked breasts of women, and also observed that 'At night [they] sleep on the wet ground coiled up like animals.'

We should understand that these weren't some kind of Neanderthal throwback. These were normal, biologically modern human beings just like us. The difference is that they had never felt the need for clothing, and so their bodies had adapted to the cold. The human body doesn't need clothes in order to survive.

Reason 2: Many activities, especially swimming, just make more sense naked. (And you might also save yourself wads of cash!)

Let's be sensible about this. We're not advocating universal mass nudity just because we don't need clothes, appealing though the idea may be. Leaving aside the legal, religious and moral obstacles there are some occasions when being clothed is definitely desirable, even crucial; bee-keeping or working in a steel foundry for instance.

But there are a surprising number of occasions when being naked simply makes more sense.

Take swimming for example.

Let's face it. The bathing suit is totally irrelevant to any activity in or under water. As Bernard Rudofsky wrote, 'it neither keeps us dry or warm and if the purpose of bathing is to get wet, the bathing suit does not make us wetter. At best, it is a social dress, like the dinner jacket.'

Neither does it aid the act of swimming. Studies carried out by the West German Olympic swim team showed that swimsuits impede movement and actually slow down a swimmer.

So why do we wear them? They're not even healthy. A bathing suit can trap creatures such as ticks and sea-lice that bite or sting but which find nowhere to hide on a naked body.

To preserve one's modesty perhaps? Well maybe, but only just. Today's male costumes are brief enough, but female bathing costumes are positively minuscule, containing less fabric than a small handkerchief. Bikini tops generally consist of little more than two postage stamps on a string, and in any case are rarely worn on European beaches. Bikini bottoms just cover the genitals but often leave the bottom exposed, which also means they don't protect you from the sun's harmful UV rays.

Yet according statistics published in 2015 by market researchers NPD Group, annual US spending on women's two-piece bathing suits totalled *eight billion US dollars,* even though The Ladies' Home Journal has estimated that 85 per cent of all swimsuits purchased never touch the water.

Doesn't make a lot of sense does it?

Before we finish with swimming, here's a little snippet that you might find interesting if you're tempted to go skinny dipping in more tropical waters. According to the experts, including specialists at the Florida Museum of Natural Museum, an all-over-tan can dramatically reduce your chances of being swallowed up by a shark!

Apparently the flashes of white skin which characterise the bodies of people who rarely expose their bodies to the sun and air help to attract a shark, and alert it to the possibility of dinner being served. An all-over tan is much less noticeable to a fishy predator, so you're significantly less likely to end up as the main course.

The moral is clear: before you go swimming in shark infested waters get naked and top up your tan!

Reason 3: Wearing clothing can seriously damage your health!

The skin is a marvellous creation. Not only is it the largest organ of our body, it always fits perfectly. It may get a bit rumpled and baggy over the years, but you know what we mean.

It stretches, it's waterproof yet not watertight. This enables it to protect our internal organs against water from the outside, whilst letting water vapour out in the form of perspiration. The skin is our body's thermostat, regulating our body temperature through the process of panting and perspiration. Amazingly, this miraculous body-part can even heal itself when damaged. However, in order to do these things in the most effective way, skin needs to be naked. Clothing just hampers its efficient operation.

In any case, some exposure of the skin to sunlight is necessary for the body to produce vitamin D, vital for, among other things, calcium absorption and a strong immune system. This is especially important for the growth of strong bones in young children. The wearing of clothes prevents the skin from absorbing vitamin D efficiently, which, as we shall see, can lead to long-term health problems.

So it seems that the body was designed to operate most efficiently in the nude. In fact, clothing can be positively dangerous to your health, because as well as preventing your body's natural resources from doing their job, clothing can actually cause illness. This is especially true of tight clothing, which is suspected of causing illness by restricting the natural flow of blood and lymphatic fluid.

According to researchers, wearing a bra can cause all manner of unpleasantness, including soreness and even breast cancer. It seems that ladies who wear bras for more than 12 hours each day except for bed are 21 times more likely to get breast cancer than those who wear bras less than 12 hours per day. Those who wear bras even in bed are 155 times more likely to get breast cancer than those who don't wear bras at all.

Don't believe us? See what the researchers at BraFree (*http://www.brafree.com*) have to say and then read '*Dressed to Kill*" and '*Get It Off*.' You'll never wear a bra again! (See the resources section for more on this research.)

And it's not only the ladies who are at risk. The same research suggests that tight underclothes may cause testicular cancer in men, as restrictive clothing is thought to impede the lymphatic system, the body's natural drainage system which amongst other things filters cancer causing toxins from the body.

And if we really want to get down and dirty, clothing (especially underclothing) harbours and encourages the growth of disease and odour-causing bacteria and yeasts which cause very unpleasant odours and—well. You get the picture.

The very latest research, although not yet endorsed by the US Food and Drugs Administration goes further.

According to experts at The California Institute of Science, skin contact with the earth, in the sense of bare flesh on grass or sand, has real, physical, measurable long-term health benefits that are necessary to our well-being. Or to put it the other way round, denying ourselves this intimate contact with earth's energy leads to a long term and potentially serious diminution of our health.

Their findings, which, it has to be said, have not yet been universally recognised, are as follows:

The earth's surface is charged with an enormous reservoir of free electrons which, in effect, means that the earth is electric.

And so are we. Every process in our bodies is regulated by finely-tuned electrical systems. However, just like, say, a TV set, we get a build-up of static in our bodies (called *emfs* - electric and magnetic fields) which if not discharged causes an accumulation within us of *free radicals*, the so-called 'molecules of inflammation' and a major cause of illness.

In the natural course of things, this static build-up is discharged by simple skin contact with the earth, which in return sends billions of free electrons (which act as antioxidants) back into the body, thus neutralising the effect of the free radicals. This is one of the miracles of nature, a perfectly designed two-way process which maintains our normal chemical reactions, keeps us healthy and has worked flawlessly for most of human history.

Unfortunately, however, over the last 60 years or so most of us in the developed world have increasingly insulated ourselves from the earth by wearing synthetically-soled shoes and inhabiting suspended-floored structures. Disconnected from the earth in this way means that we are no longer able to discharge our static energy, which leads to a build-up of emfs and an electrical imbalance which helps grow and sustain free radicals.

Cardiovascular disease, diabetes, multiple sclerosis, asthma, arthritis, gastrointestinal disorders and hypertension are all linked to stress, inflammation and free radicals, and it's no coincidence that each of these diseases has sky-rocketed over the last 50-60 years, *the same length of time that we've become insulated from the earth.*

Fortunately, the remedy is as easy as taking off your shoes, socks or stockings and walking or standing barefoot on the earth. Better still, sit or lie naked on the earth for a while everyday This allows a natural flow of electrons to and from our bodies and connects us to the vital earth rhythms that set many of our biological clocks. (For a concise and fascinating exploration of this subject we recommend *Earthing Therapy:*

Nature's Most Powerful Natural Health Secret by James Edgar. See Resources section.)

It's a complex and compelling proposition which is still being investigated by the medical profession, but whatever the eventual verdict it's a great excuse to lie naked on the beach for an hour or two.

Reason 4: You get lots of fresh air and exercise

Despite the fact that many of us have to practice much of our naturism indoors, it is essentially an outdoor recreation. At its most basic it gives us the opportunity to breath fresh clean air and to expose our skin to the benign influence of the elements for a time, a practice which for generations we've believed was good for us. More recently however, concerns about the effects of ozone depletion and atmospheric pollution on our heath have cast doubt on this idea. We have been advised to treat the great outdoors with caution and to avoid direct sunlight if possible. This has been very embarrassing and not a little inconvenient for nudists, for whom the benefits of solar exposure was a prime raison d'être.

Now, thankfully, newer findings have spared our blushes and vindicated our beliefs. Traditional wisdom was, it seems, right all along.

Recent research has suggested an inverse relationship between solar exposure and osteoporosis, rectal and colon cancer, breast cancer, and even the most deadly form of skin cancer, malignant melanoma. In fact, some experts believe that the incidence of some cancers may be reduced by 30 to 40 per cent *by sensible* sun exposure. (Note the word sensible. More about that later.)

According to these findings ultraviolet B rays, the rays that give you sunburn and which until now have been considered so dangerous, interact with a special cholesterol in unprotected skin. Once stimulated, this cholesterol triggers your liver and kidneys to make vitamin D3. Now vitamin D3 isn't really a vitamin, but rather a type of steroid hormone that can drastically improve your immune system function. Vitamin D3 also controls cellular growth and helps you absorb calcium from your digestive tract. Most importantly, this hormone/vitamin inhibits the growth of cancer cells.

Conversely, if we block out the sun's ultraviolet B rays—the rays that trigger the production of the cancer inhibiting vitamin D3—we increase our chances of contracting the disease.

And guess what? Most recommended daily sunscreens are designed to block ultraviolet B rays!

So, just what is going on here? For years we've been told to stay out of the sun because overexposure can be fatal. Now, it seems, this may be bad advice. So is our sun phobia actually doing more harm than good?

Dr. Richard Hobday, author of 'The Healing Sun' firmly believes so. According to his research, the number of people who die from breast cancer, colon cancer, prostate cancer, ovarian cancer, heart disease, multiple sclerosis and osteoporosis—all diseases which could benefit from sunlight—is far greater than the number of deaths from skin cancer.

Another researcher, Dr Gordon Ainsleigh of California agrees. After meticulously reviewing 50 years of medical literature on cancer, he concludes that, 'the benefits of regular sun exposure outweigh the risks of squamous-basal skin cancer, accelerated ageing and melanoma.'

In 2010 The British Medical Journal published research that indicated that people who have high levels of vitamin D, the main source of which is sunlight through skin exposure, are less likely to develop bowel cancer than those with low levels.

Explaining the findings, the science programme manager for the World Cancer Research Fund said 'This is the biggest ever study on this subject and there is now quite a lot of evidence from studying populations that people who have low levels of vitamin D are more likely to develop bowel cancer.'

Yet another researcher, investigating the specific link between solar rays and breast cancer, has calculated that 55 women die from *underexposure* to the sun to every one that dies of overexposure.

So, now we have two conflicting pieces of advice. On the one hand the official line is still that we should protect ourselves against the sun, whilst the latest research indicates that the exact opposite is true.

So what are we to make of this? Are the two things mutually exclusive? Well, we don't think so. Remember that the new research talks about *sensible* exposure, and therein lies the key. You must use common sense.

To roast yourself for hours when the sun is at its most powerful is just plain stupid. So is getting paranoid about the great outdoors and shutting yourself in a darkened room during the daylight hours.

But to bathe awhile in the rays of the early and late sun, and to feel the air on your naked skin—now that's what we call sensible!

Exercise

Games such as miniten (a form of tennis unique, as far as we know, to naturism), volleyball and squash are almost universally played at landed clubs, whilst the larger sites may have their own swimming pools and saunas.

If you don't feel like indulging in anything too energetic, pétanque (boules) and croquet are also very popular nudist activities. And if even these gentle pastimes are a little too stressful for you, you can always take a restful stroll around the grounds. This is a particular pleasure of ours and one of our own favourite nudist activities is to walk naked with friends through the woods in a soft, gentle, warm rainfall, with the droplets splashing on the leaves and refreshing our bodies. It's also a great stress-buster—twice as good as meditation and not so boring!

Although you'll find plenty of opportunities for exercise if you want it, there is no pressure to take part. If you just want to hang out and talk, or read or play cards, or just sit quiet and meditate, nobody will mind. But if you want to get some exercise whilst getting fresh air to your lungs and body, there is definitely nothing to beat naturism!

The Mental Benefits

Reason 5: You'll liberate your mind and body

If you were to ask any group of naturist to define the single most important benefit to be obtained from naturism, our guess is that nearly all of them would give as their first answer, *a sense of freedom and liberation.*

We would agree. There is really no feeling to equal the elation you feel when you shed your clothes and expose your body to the sun and air for the first time. After a lifetime of clothes oppression, the feeling of exhilaration and liberation is almost overwhelming.

Although it is at its most powerful the first few times you strip off, the feeling never really leaves you. No matter how long you remain a naturist, you will never, ever, lose that magical sense of release, every time you remove your clothes in a naturist environment. In the over-organised, constrained world in which we live today, where it's becoming more and more difficult to find a true sense of liberty, nudism offers a delightful and simple path to freedom.

Reason 6: You'll increase your self-esteem

We all like to feel that we are somehow special, that there is a certain uniqueness about us that sets us apart from our fellow beings. We like to think that we are fiercely independent, free-thinking and able to make our own judgements according to our own criteria. We may even enjoy thinking of ourselves as being a little radical.

Sadly, most of us rarely live up to our own self-image.

In a tightly managed society, thinking for oneself is applauded and superficially encouraged, but rarely appreciated. And for good reason; highly organised societies cannot work if too many citizens think outside the box. Advanced social orders rely on a compliant population in order to function properly. A questioning, independent-thinking public would gum up the machinery of state, and the nation would grind to a halt.

Cynical as this sounds, it is nonetheless true, and so from the cradle to the grave we are moulded into the shape that 'they' want us to be, purely for the convenience of the state. We are pressured to conform, and few of us dare to explore the exciting new possibilities that may await us if we stray beyond the official line.

But naturists are different. They have dared to step over the line towards the only freedom that really counts—freedom of the mind.

Taking the decision to try naturism for the first time forces you to make a gigantic intellectual leap—perhaps the biggest of your life. You have to overcome a lifetime of conditioning which has taught you that nudity is shameful and indecent. This isn't an easy mental shift to make, even when common sense tells you that there is nothing remotely sinful about honest nudity. But if you have the courage to follow your instincts and really go for it then things will never be the same again.

Discovering that you *can* do your own thing is tremendously empowering, and enhances your perception of yourself as a truly independent person. Even if you choose not to proclaim your nudism to the world, or you eventually become a 'lapsed' nudist, you will have proved to yourself that you, at least, are an individual capable of making up your own mind, whatever pressures convention places upon you.

Naturism alters the way that you look at yourself, and the world. Forever. Almost uniquely it gives you the opportunity to discover true freedom of both body and mind. It is the supreme form of self-expression.

And if there were no other reason to try naturism, then this alone would be reason enough.

Reason 7: You'll have less hang-ups, and a more rounded view of life

If studies are to be believed, a lack of confidence in one's body-image is one of the more frequent complexes afflicting people in the western world, and is linked to such serious and debilitating illnesses as Body Dysmorphic Disorder, Anorexia Nervosa, Bulimia Nervosa, Depression and Binge Eating Disorder. One body-image study found that 33 per cent of men and an astonishing 75 per cent of women were dissatisfied with their physiques. In a recent poll by People Magazine, 80 per cent of women reported that the images of women on TV, the movies and in fashion magazine advertising made them feel insecure about their looks. In addition, the poll indicated that women are made to feel so insecure that 34 per cent are willing to try diets that pose health risks, 34 per cent are willing to go 'under the knife', and 93 per cent indicated they had made various and repeated attempts to lose weight to measure up to the images.

This isn't surprising. Most people don't often see other people naked, and when they do the nudity is usually on-screen, on-stage or on-page, and portrayed by actresses or actors with perfect bodies—sometimes impossibly so, with enhanced bits and pieces that owe more to the surgeon's knife or the photographer's skill than to Mother Nature. Because of this, these faultless bodies become the standard against which they measure themselves, usually to their own detriment.

Ladies worry that their breasts are too small, or too large, or that their tummy is wrinkly or their bottom saggy. Men worry that their penis is too small (rarely that it's too large), or that their beer-belly is ugly or their body-hair unattractive.

Thus, they go through life with an inadequate body-image, convinced of their own unsightliness and lack, victims of a quest for an illusory physical perfection which very few obtain, and then only fleetingly.

And yet just one visit to a nudist beach would allay this hang-up forever, because by contrast, nudists have no such anxieties. Studies have shown that naturists experience considerably less torment about their own body image than their textile brethren. Although they may wish for a better body, (and a greater percentage of nudists than textiles spend time working out precisely because their body is on show more often), they accept it as it is, imperfections and all, and just get on with enjoying themselves.

Consequently, if you cast your eyes round a typical nudist beach or resort, you may see the odd 'perfect ten' but we'll guarantee that they'll be in the minority. Most will be, well, just ordinary. Fat, thin, short, tall, some with bigger bits, some with smaller bits and some with bits missing altogether. There is no such thing as *the norm*, and no one cares anyway. We can promise you that whatever you look like you won't look out of place on a nudist beach.

Ironically, the only people whose bodies are likely to match the current stereotype of the body-beautiful often fall victim to a more insidious inhibition. Younger people frequently have flawless physiques, but lack the confidence to defy the social pressure to conform. This is one reason for the so-called missing generation of nudists that is such a worry for the naturist movement. Our own experience indicates that this situation arises when youngsters are introduced to nudism when well into puberty rather than at an earlier age, and the only answer is to wait until they get older and more confident. The problem can be avoided, however, if the young are initiated into nudism from the very beginning. Young people have to suffer enough neuroses as it is; one less complex can only be a good thing!

There's one more point, which the more perceptive of you may already have picked up. We assert here that naturists experience considerably less anguish about their own body-image than textiles. This is based on studies carried out by Dr Marilyn Story. (*Comparisons of Body Self-Concept between Social Nudists and Nonnudists. Journal of Psychology 118.1 September, 1984*). However, the research doesn't establish whether nudists have less of a body-image problem because they are naturally attracted to naturism in the first place, or whether the physical practice of nudism tends to ease the anxiety over time.

Does this weaken our case? Not one bit. Either way, the naturist is more at home with his or her body than most textiles. So please come and join us, and get rid of one more hang-up!

Reason 8: You'll experience a greater sense of belonging

Loneliness is one of the most insidious diseases of modern times. It is not the same as being alone; it's possible for people to feel isolated even in a crowd. It can affect the young and old, rich and poor, its effects can be life threatening, and sadly it's a malaise that appears to be on the increase. It's not our intention to discuss roots and causes, but to make the point that in our society many people feel alienated, and lack a sense of belonging and of being a part of a larger group which is an important and immensely reassuring emotion which we all need.

And which naturism provides in a most unique and comprehensive way.

Belonging to and being accepted into a naturist group offers a particularly strong sense of kinship. Although there are many other communities that one can belong to—the golf club, the local history society, even the UFO spotters club for instance—there exists a very special camaraderie within the nudist movement.

It's not that naturism is a closed or secret society, which is a condition that always tends to lead to a greater rapport between members. No. The uniqueness of the bonding lies in the nature of nudism itself. Your fellow nudists are prepared to bestow upon you a privilege usually reserved for one's closest partner—that of seeing themselves and their loved ones naked. What greater honour, short of sleeping with you, could someone offer you? And how much more affinity could you have with them?

And the fellowship is not just reserved for the times when you are naked. Meeting someone in a normal social situation, once you have spent time with them nude in a naturist environment, engenders a unique accord. Like illicit lovers meeting at a party, you will share a secret, something that 'the others' don't. It confers a very special sense of belonging.

You may be naked, but you won't be naked and alone.

The Social Benefits

Reason 9: Re-connect with the environment

'We are dysfunctional socially and environmentally because we are

cut off and isolated from the world of nature and the natural.' Albert Gore.

We all know that most of us have drifted to an unhealthy extent away from our natural environment.

And that such a separation is psychologically, spiritually and physically damaging to us and disastrous to the environment.

Nudism provides a fabulous opportunity to reconnect with the environment in a unique and enormously gratifying way. In fact, even we hard-bitten old veteran nudists can testify that being naked within nature is an unusually uplifting, indeed, almost spiritual experience. At first you feel self-conscious, then a little vulnerable, and then you experience such an overwhelming sense of belonging that some first-timers have been known to cry with emotion. It's true. We've seen it ourselves. And if you think that they must have been over-reacting, we can only urge you to try it for yourself, because it is a feeling that is almost impossible to explain. You are no longer an intruder, an alien in the landscape; you have become part of it. You have come home.

From this perspective the natural world around you takes on an almost psychedelic quality of colour, sights, sounds and sensations. The fresh air and sunshine—or perhaps the refreshing rain—touches your bare flesh in an almost sensual way. The sounds of nature are amplified and reach you with a previously unheard clarity. You will smell the earth and the world around you like never before. And beneath your feet, the rich earth connects you to the elements from which you sprang. In our more spiritual moments we like to think that this state of heightened perception is Mother Nature's way of thanking us for re-joining Her on Her own terms, but we're probably just being fanciful.

But then again, maybe not.

Although not all environmentalists are nudists, most nudists are environmentalists to a greater or lesser extent. They share many of the same aims, and the Nudist Charter goes so far as to incorporate a respect for the environment in its wording. Naturists on the whole take their green responsibilities seriously; most member clubs do not have a litter problem for instance, and the lighting of fires, building work, waste-management and ground-clearance schemes are usually carefully thought out and tightly managed to minimise environmental impact.

There are some nudists who argue that the very act of not wearing clothes itself has a positive impact on the ecosystem. They point out that the processes involved in manufacturing and cleaning clothes are detrimental to the environment, and that the more we can do without our garments the less damage we do.

Although we can see the logic behind this argument, (and it's backed up with some impressive statistics—see our e-book *205 Arguments for Naturism* which can be downloaded from our nudist blog at *http://snipurl.com/bacher2*), we personally think it's stretching the environmental proposition a little thin. Such an infinitesimal proportion of the world's population are nudists, and for such a tiny percentage of their time, that the effect must be unnoticeable. When the entire world gets naked we'll see the difference, but until then nudists will carry on as always, quietly respecting, and re-connecting with the environment.

Reason 10: You get to meet lots of nice people

Genuine nudists are very nice people.

We would say that wouldn't we, but it happens to be true. Many of our best friends are nudists, and of the thousands of naturists that we've met over the years, we can think of only three individuals—yes just three—who were disagreeable, and only one of those significantly so. This is an astonishing percentage compared to any other walk of life or social activity, and there can only be three explanations:

We are so wonderful that everyone falls in love with us! Nice thought, but come on, let's get real. Besides, if we're so special how come every nudist has the same experience?

We've just been incredibly lucky. Possibly, but no one gets that lucky, and, to repeat the previous point, we can't *all* have been so lucky.

Which leaves us with the inescapable conclusion that genuine nudists are just very nice people.

Quite why this should be so is difficult to say. Naturists are normal, morally responsible respectable citizens—singles, couples and families—who just happen to share a passion for wholesome social nudity, but the same could be said for any other group of people with a different shared interest. What makes nudists especially nice remains a mystery. Perhaps nudism attracts the pleasantest individuals in the first place, or maybe the practice of nudism somehow improves people. Who knows? And really, who cares? Let's just enjoy the situation.

It's an overworked example, but it's none-the-less true, that you can leave an unlocked car at a nudist resort and nothing will be taken. Nudist resorts and beaches tend to be orderly, well behaved places.

Even at a nudist holiday city such as Cap d'Agde, containing some 40 thousand people at the height of the season, there is none of the threatening atmosphere, violence and general loutishness that disfigure other holiday hot-spots. Any sort of crime is almost non-existent, and most large complexes, including the gigantic Cap d'Agde, need no more than minimal security.

You can't say that about Benidorm, Bondi or Palm Springs.

Given the nature of nudism, we would be breathtakingly naive if we didn't suspect that there are in our midst those whose motives are less than genuine. However, these aren't real nudists and they are rooted out as soon as their activities become suspicious. We've more to say about these creatures later.

Fortunately these cases are few and far between, but regrettably they attract adverse publicity out of all proportion to their importance, and have helped tarnish the image of naturists in the eyes of the unbelievers. Don't be put off by such lurid hype, and discover for yourself how delightful real naturists can be.

Reason 11: You get to go to lots of fabulous places

It's a common misconception that naturist sites are primitive, back-to-nature, make-do-and-mend places in remote woodland without modern amenities or comfort—or else they're like the 1950s military style holiday camps with which UK readers of a certain age will be familiar. To be honest, such a view is not without some justification; until quite recently the standard of most nudist facilities was, frankly, awful, and it's a tribute to the commitment of earlier generations of nudists that they continued to patronise and support the movement despite such meagre resources. Even today such places exist, but they are becoming the exception rather than the rule, and thankfully times are changing.

As nudist holidays have become part of the mainstream vacation industry demand has grown for more up-market amenities. Today's holidaymakers demand high standards of comfort with facilities to match, and nudist destinations are no exception. Resort owners and developers are taking notice, and we are now seeing the emergence of exclusive nudist resorts set on fabulous beaches which can match the comfort and quality of almost any textile resort anywhere on earth.

And not just on the earth. If water is more your thing, you've a great choice of superb nautical nudist holidays to choose from, from crewing a schooner through the Aegean to enjoying an all-inclusive nude vacation on a luxury cruise-liner around the Caribbean or the Mediterranean. One major nudist vacation company has even pioneered the nudist river cruise, hosting a nude luxury river voyage down the Rhone River in the South of France in July 2010.

If going by ship doesn't float your boat, why not try flying nude to your destination? In 2009 a nudist travel agency chartered a nudist plane so that its clients could begin their nudist holiday without delay by stripping off as soon as the plane reached its cruising altitude. Although the nude flights are not available at the time of writing, the company assures us that they were a great success and may well offer them again in the future. It seems that nudist holidays have—if you'll pardon us—really taken off!

Reason 12: Because it's fun!

And what better reason could there be for doing anything?

4

Where To Go Bare

Happily there are today hundreds, if not thousands, of places where you can safely go naked, and that's not including your back garden! They fall into five main categories.

Nudist Beaches

Sauna and swimming groups

Nudist vacations, resorts and centres

Internet and Special Interest Groups (SIGs)

Nudist Beaches

(In this section the term nude beaches also applies to lakesides, rivers, bathing holes and similar locations.)

This is the easiest, no hassle, 100 per cent successful way to go nude. These locations are usually freely accessible to the general public at most times, require no membership card, have no quota system (see chapter 8), and are free of controls except those required by good behaviour, common sense, custom, and the law of the land. These are definitely the best places to go for your first taste of nudism.

You don't need to book, you can just turn up. You can go as often as you want and stay as long as you like. You don't even have to strip off if you don't want to. (Although you should, if possible. See the section on Etiquette, chapter 14.)

There are very few countries in which nudism is practiced that don't have nude beaches, and in the holiday hot-spots you might find some absolute gems. As long as you can find your way there you'll always be able to indulge your taste for communal nudism.

There are three different types of nude beaches. In each case, the nude areas tend to be separated from the non-nude areas by notices and signs to prevent conflicts. Do your research first, and be sure you know what type of beach you're visiting. These are your three options:

Official nude beaches

These have been sanctioned by the authorities and can be freely used (within certain limits) without fear of prosecution. Very often the designated nudist area is a defined stretch of a larger beach. These are your safest choices.

Nude beaches that are *tolerated* by the authorities

These are areas that are used for nude recreation but are not officially sanctioned for such activity. The authorities customarily turn a blind eye to the nudists, but may decide to take a less indulgent view at any time. These can be risky.

Beaches where nudity is illegal, and nude people risk a fine or worse

These are best avoided, especially in countries where nudity is not popular.

Some advantages of using nude beaches

- No waiting list to become a member.
- No complicated joining procedure. You don't have to give out personal details on an application form.
- No quota system (see chapter 8) making it an ideal option for single men.
- You don't have to work your butt off on workdays.
- You don't have to book or reserve a place. You can turn up when you want, stay as long as you want and leave when you want.

- No rules or regulations except for the law of the land, local bye-laws and the requirements of good citizenship.
- No waiting outside a gate in the middle of nowhere, honking your car horn or ringing a bell until someone opens up for you.
- A large, constantly changing group of people to mix with.
- It's FREE!

Some disadvantages of using nude beaches.

- Misunderstanding the legal status of the beach could land you in jail!
- Unrestricted and unregulated access means there's a greater chance that voyeurs, perverts, sneak cameramen and other undesirables may be amongst you. Do you really want your nude photo plastered over the internet? And don't let the kids out of your sight!
- A large, constantly changing group of people might make it difficult to make friends easily.
- Usually little in the way of amenities.

Sauna and swimming groups

These offer a good opportunity for regular nudist activity when it's inconvenient to go to the club or beach, for instance during the winter months. Usually privately run, they tend to be small mixed groups from a particular locality which meet on a regular basis to use a swimming baths or similar facility.

They are rarely clubs in the strictest sense of the word, but more an informal gathering of friends and acquaintances who have either been invited or introduced by existing members. They are widespread throughout the nudist world and there is likely to be one near you. Ask your national nudist association for details.

Nudist vacations, resorts and centres

These range from the small members' club with a trailer for hire and the most basic amenities to the huge Cap d'Agde complex in France, with every conceivable shape, size and standard of comfort in between. Some of the newer resorts boast a fabulous degree of luxuriousness, and the increasingly popular nudist cruises are also of an extremely high standard. A nudist vacation can be a good introduction to naturism for the newbie nudist, being a one-off which needn't be repeated if nudism proves not to be to your liking.

Be warned, though, that some are more suitable for the first timer than others. Cap d'Agde, for instance is often touted as an ideal sampler for novices, but we don't agree. Although we personally like the place, the racy ambience that it assumes after dark is not typical of real-life club nudism and can give inexperienced naturists the wrong impression of what to expect from everyday naturism. For the same reason we don't recommend it for children.

Unfortunately the expense in terms of time, money and travel usually precludes enjoying the resorts as your regular, main nudist experience, but we'd certainly recommend that you consider them as an introduction to the wider world of nudism.

Internet and Special Interest Groups (SIGs)

The advent of the World Wide Web has given rise to a plethora of online nudist groups including nudist dating sites, beach-user groups, Yahoo communities, discussion groups, news groups and all manner of forums and message-boards run by the thousands of individual nudist web sites in cyberspace. An internet search for *online nudist groups* or similar will bring up hundreds of possibilities. The thing that nearly all of these have in common is that they are usually very easy to join, require little more than a computer with an internet connection and can be accessed without leaving your home. You can't always be sure who you're talking to though, so always take care to protect your privacy and do be wary of the so-called nudist chat rooms and web-cam rooms as many of these have become little more than amateur porn sites.

Another fairly recent development are the naturist special interest groups (SIGs), which are simply groups of naturists who share a passion within naturism, such as such as gay nudists, Christian Nudists, nude cyclists, wild naked swimming, nude bungee jumpers, nude yoga (including one group splendidly named YogaBare), and just-about-anything really.

Some of the most popular SIG activities include:

Nude Dining

Nude dining is surprisingly popular, and there are several groups and even one or two commercial companies devoted to this, with venues ranging from private homes to city centre restaurants and cruise boats in New York harbour hired exclusively for the event.

If the idea of nude dining tickles your fancy then go ahead and try it. You won't get arrested and at least you're likely to get a good meal. But do try to avoid the soup—it burns when you drop it down your bare bosom.

Nude Hiking

Nude hiking is the nudist desire to be naked in nature taken one stage farther. The nude hiker moves beyond the beach or the resort and goes out into the wild places of the earth. (And some not so remote. There is at least one UK group that wanders the overpopulated English countryside in the buff!)

Nude hiking enthusiasts claim that it is a totally cathartic experience, the essence of being naked in nature and of reconnecting with Mother Earth, and as someone who experiences an emotional thrill whenever I get naked amongst the woods of my own little nudist paradise I can identify with that.

The difference is, of course that my little Eden is private. The remote places of the earth, though admittedly uncrowded, are not. Which means that unless you are very vigilant and careful you may run into someone who may be offended by your nudity, which in most jurisdictions, transforms your harmless communion with nature into an offence, punishable under the law.

It does have many devotees however, and very few of them report any problems with other hikers.

It is of course an extremely easy activity to do, given a reasonable level of fitness and a stout pair of walking boots. Just go somewhere remote, strip off, start walking, and hope that no one sees you. You don't even have to enjoy it with like-minded souls; if you don't know anybody who wants to share it with you just go on your own. It is the ideal solo nude activity, although those in the know don't recommend this. There is safety in numbers on any sort of wilderness activity, and in the case of nude hiking startled textile hikers are less likely to feel threatened by a naked rambler if the nude one is with a— preferably mixed-gender—group.

Here's a few more tips from the experts:

- Hike on weekdays, when you are less likely to encounter other hikers.
- Avoid trails which are popular with families.
- Study the area well before you go, and tell someone where you'll be.
- Take everything and more that you are likely to need.
- Be sensible in the elements.

Nude hiking and rambling is not exactly mainstream naturism, but it does have a small and enthusiastic following. You should easily find some guidance, and even join a group. It is probably not legal, but unless you are unlucky enough to run into someone who complains you're unlikely to be arrested.

Nude Gardening

Why garden nude? Gosh, whyever not? To quote from *The World Naked Gardening Day* website, (*http://wngd.org/*)

'Our culture needs to move toward a healthy sense of both body acceptance and our relation to the natural environment. Gardening naked is not only a simple joy, it reminds us – even if only for those few sun-kissed minutes - that we can be honest with who we are as humans and as part of this planet.'

Nude gardening is second only to swimming on the list of family-friendly activities that people would consider doing nude. At least two books have been published on the subject and it boasts its very own annual *World Naked Gardening Day.*

Despite its attraction, and its inclusion here as an SIG, it's not a group activity in the conventional sense of the word. Most folks who garden nude (myself included) do so in the privacy of their own garden, and those gardening SIGs that do exist are low key and very local so you may be hard pressed to find an actual nude gardening group to join.

However, if you keep your eyes open you will find communal nude gardening events that you can join, and you can always visit somewhere like the home of *The Naked Gardeners* Ian & Barbara Pollard at Abbey House Gardens, near Malmesbury, Wiltshire, UK (*http://www.abbeyhousegardens.co.uk/*) for inspiration and contacts.

Alternatively you can start your own naturist garden SIG. Make sure your garden is as private as possible, get naked and get gardening. Let your friends and family know what you're doing, invite them to join you and maybe you will start that club after all! If nothing else you'll get help with the garden chores. Just watch out for the rosebushes.

Nude Canoeing

More common in the USA than elsewhere, nude canoeing is another very popular activity, with several SIGs devoted to it. Unless you're paddling on private waters, many of the caveats given in the hiking section apply here also, however because you are sat in a canoe for most of the time the fact that you are naked isn't immediately obvious (especially if you're male), to unsuspecting passers-by so you may be less likely to get into trouble. You won't have to sit for hours in soggy clothes either.

Nudist Photography

With the nude being such a perennial favourite of photographers, you'll not be surprised that there is at least one SIG about nudist photography.

However, here we're not talking about *nude* photography but *nudist* photography, where both models and photographers are naked. The idea is that every one takes it in turns to be photographer and subject, so that all have an equal opportunity to develop their hobby and there's no need to pay for models. For best results you need a good mix of gender and ages, but I understand that this isn't always the case and some some sessions may not always live up to expectations.

There are many nudist SIGs to choose from and they offer something for almost everyone, but, as ever on the internet, do be careful about what you're getting into.

The Nudist Club.

The nudist club, in the form of the private landed club is in many ways the mainstay of the naturist movement and is what most people imagine when they think about nudism.

Oddly enough, some of the most popular perceptions of a 'nudist colony' are not too far from the truth. The woodland glade behind the gate, the ball game, the middle-aged guy with a paunch and bald patch, even the voluptuous babe, all are common features of most of the smaller clubs which account for the majority of nudist real estate.

Landed clubs are usually designed to be small oases of peace and quiet where like-minded individuals can strip off and enjoy each other's company in congenial surroundings, safe from prying eyes and the threat of legal action. They're places to get naked and relax, or talk, or play games, or walk, or just re-connect with nature and generally leave the outside world and its woes behind, just for a while. They are miniature communities which engender a definite sense of belonging and at their best they are the most refreshing places you'll ever find. We wholeheartedly recommend that you join at least one.

Landed clubs vary in size from something just larger than a suburban lawn to large, multi-acre estates with all the mod-cons, and offer amenities to suit all requirements and expectations, depending on your taste and how much you're prepared to pay for membership.

There are two types: the privately-owned club and the member-owned club.

Privately owned clubs

Privately owned clubs belong to an individual or company who is responsible for the running, maintenance and development of the club and its facilities. Although as a paying member you will have little say in the running of the place, you need do nothing but turn up and enjoy yourself. Remember though that these clubs exist to make a profit for the owners and therefore can be quite expensive. The upside of this, however, is that it's a competitive market and in order to attract and keep members they need to offer a continually high standard of facilities.

Member owned clubs

The members club by contrast is, as the name implies, owned and run by its members. It may have been purchased by them from a private owner but more usually it owes its existence to a group of committed individuals who have banded together, raised the finance, bought or rented the land, obtained the necessary permissions and started the ball rolling. Management is by an elected committee, backed up by a board of trustees (usually the original founders, or senior long-time members) who deal with legal issues.

Subscriptions to a members club are usually very much cheaper than those of a private club, and as a paid up member you will have a say in the running of the club. Depending on the club constitution you may also be entitled to a share of the proceeds should the club be wound up and the assets sold. However, you will also be expected to contribute in some way to the maintenance and development of the club, which means attending work days, fund raising events, helping to plan and build new amenities and so on; it's not all about lazing in the sun.

Also remember that all costs have to be paid out of the revenue generated by and from the members themselves, and if the membership base is small or the fees are minimal there might not be enough in the pot to achieve anything more than ongoing basic maintenance, which will leave nothing to spend on providing amenities. Whether you choose a larger, more expensive club with extensive facilities or whether you go for a much quieter and cheaper club with the most basic amenities is a choice only you can make.

Another type of members' club is the non-landed club, which doesn't have grounds of its own but whose members regularly meet at different locations specially hired for the occasion, or enjoy group visits to landed clubs. Some swim-sauna and internet groups also fall into this category.

Some advantages of joining a nudist club

- You'll be part of a community. Meeting others regularly makes it easy to make lasting friendships.
- The vetting and screening measures mean that you're more likely to meet real nudists and less likely to meet real fruitcakes.
- Clubs and sites are usually well managed and run with care. They are often cleaner and better tended than beaches, and less likely to experience outbreaks of bad behaviour. The owners, or the committee and members have a financial interest (ie. the membership fee) in ensuring that things stay that way.
- At a privately owned club you can turn up and just relax. No maintenance chores.
- At a member owned club, you will have a say in how the club is run, and, if you're elected to the committee, a chance to help run it.
- You're more likely to find amenities such as restaurants, hot tubs, pools, bars and evening entertainment at a nudist club.
- Clubs will usually be well screened for privacy.
- There may be opportunities to travel with a club group to different clubs, sites and even holiday resorts. This could be a major attraction if you're on your own.

- It's legal! No need to keep a lookout for the local law enforcement and no fear of getting a fine—or worse!

Some disadvantages of joining a Nudist Club.
- You may find it difficult to locate a club convenient for you.
- There is a membership charge, which can be expensive.
- Once you've paid your membership fee you'll be unlikely to get a refund if you change your mind.
- The more amenities available on site, the more expensive the subscription will be.
- At a member owned club you will be expected to do your share of the work.
- The nature of a nudist club means that there is a requirement to go through a membership application system and pay a fee, which can be an involved process and is a disincentive to some folk. We explain a typical signing up procedure in chapter 13 'Taking the Plunge.'

So now you know. Wherever you are in the western world there is somewhere for you to get naked. You've just got to go and find it!

5

Does Naturism Equal Sex?

They're all at it, aren't they?

That nudism and sex go hand in hand is probably the most widely held of all of the myths about naturism. It, more than any other reason, is responsible for the suspicion with which nudists are viewed by the public and, as a consequence, the secrecy in which they veil themselves.

It's particularly galling for genuine nudists—who are as morally upstanding as anyone—to be perceived in the public mind as sexual deviants, but it's not entirely surprising given the prevailing social attitude to nudity. Ironically, we nudists must share some of the blame ourselves.

Before we go any further, it might be enlightening to briefly examine the reasons behind such a widespread misconception. These are:

- The prevailing attitude towards naturism.
- The hijacking of the terms *nudist* and *naturist* by sex groups.

Let's look at them in turn.

Prevailing Attitudes

Firstly, as we've seen, thousands of years of social conditioning have instilled in society the unshakeable conviction that nudity and sex are inextricably linked. There's an old saying that goes 'there are only two things you can do with your clothes off—and the second is to take a bath!' Now we nudists (and hopefully by now, you too,) know different, but this hoary old chestnut does illustrate how widespread and deeply ingrained the belief that nudism and sex are two parts of one whole has become.

Similarly, the same conditioning teaches us that being seen naked is naughty and that allowing others to see you and your partner nude somehow indicates that you are inviting them to share in a little naughtiness, or are making yourselves 'available' to them.

This reasoning is of course nonsense—try asking me if I'm available, if you don't mind a poke in the eye—but it is a result of generations of anti-nudity brainwashing, and without a serious and costly programme of education by the nudist movement it will be with us for some time yet.

The second reason for the common belief that nudism equals sex stems from the activities of the sex-on-the-beach brigade.

Confusion with sex groups

There is no doubt that some groups and individuals who call themselves nudists are in reality swingers, swappers, voyeurs, exhibitionists and, worst of all, paedophiles.

But let's be quite clear—these people are not nudists or naturists at all, but sexually motivated individuals who use the terms to mask the purely carnal nature of their activities. Sadly, these are also the people who gain the most publicity, and when yet another 'naturist' club is exposed as a sex and swingers rendezvous the general public nudge each other knowingly, satisfied that their suspicions and their prejudices have once more been justified.

The problem is compounded by the fact that both groups use the terms nudist and naturist; the genuine nudists who used them first and the swinging set who later appropriated them (presumably because they were too embarrassed to call themselves swingers, exhibitionists or wife-swappers).

This is most evident on the internet, where adult sites routinely include *naturist* and *nudist* as descriptive keywords, resulting in any search for these terms pulling up thousands of pornographic websites. Sadly the public, unwilling or unable to distinguish between the two groups and with their inbuilt prejudices reinforced by titillating news-bytes, tend to class all nudists or naturists in the latter group.

OK. Now we've seen how and why the nudism equals sex connection has arisen and has proven so durable, let's ask the question again.

Does nudism mean sex?

Quite simply, no, nudism does NOT mean the same thing as sex.

Remember our definition of naturism?

Naturism is the enjoyment of getting as naked as possible, wherever appropriate, alone or with others, just for its own sake.

Let's repeat. *Getting naked for its own sake.* Not as a form of, or as a prelude to, sex.

This is not because nudists are anti-sexual, a-sexual, puritan or prudish. We are human, and enjoy life's little pleasures to the full.

But the practice of social nudity is an end in itself; getting naked is the whole point of it, and the nudity does not have to be justified by sexual activity.

So, let's spell it out once and for all.

The genuine nudist's attitude to sex is no different from that of the average person, ie. that it is natural and healthy and should be fully enjoyed. However, just like the average non-nudist, we believe that one's sex life is one's own private affair; it is no more acceptable to publicly discuss, practise or display it within a nudist environment than it would be in front of your textile friends, neighbours or workmates in any other situation.

Nudists are not sex-maniacs but normal people who indulge in social nudity. Nudist venues are places where we indulge in social nudity, not public sex. Contrary to popular belief, being with other naked people in a true naturist environment is not sexually stimulating and at most genuine nudist sites you will not or must not:

- Be sexually propositioned—or proposition others—in any way.
- See other individuals or couples indulging in overt sexual activity.
- Be allowed to indulge in overt sexual activity yourself.
- See—or deliberately display— an erection.
- Position or display yourself in a way that could be classed as provocative or obscene.

All clear?

Now, as we've pointed out, nudists face the same urges and temptations as everyone else and it's entirely likely that some genuine nudists are also swingers. But secret swingers exist in every social group. It's probable, for instance, that somewhere amongst the entire membership of all the golf clubs in the world there are people who are also wife-swappers. But it would be quite absurd to label all golfers as wife-swappers and every golf club as a swingers paradise on the basis of the extra-curricula exertions of a few golfers who also like to exchange partners.

So why should nudists be treated differently?

It is, however, worth pointing out that even within the ranks of the genuine (ie. non-sexually motivated) clubs there are different ideas of what is acceptable and what is not.

On the one hand some clubs are so fearful of attracting the vaguest suspicion of impropriety that they have adopted an almost puritanical attitude to personal interaction, forbidding even mild forms of affection such as hand-holding or cheek-pecking.

Other clubs however, whilst never quite overstepping the bounds of decency take a more robust view, allowing certain expressions of intimacy and even staging risqué events such as lingerie parties and nude beauty contests. Thankfully most clubs fall somewhere in between and if you've strong views either way you should check exactly what the policy of the club is before you join.

So, there we have it. Nudism and sex are not the same. Official. End of story. And if you still don't believe us, try it for yourself!

Just for the record here are some final thoughts on the subject of naturism and sex.

Getting naked to practice social nudity for its own sake is a definition of nudism-naturism as it is practised by nudists-naturists.

Getting naked as aid or a prelude to sex is a definition of foreplay. Those who do this in groups are swingers, not nudists. We do not judge their lifestyle. We just wish they'd call themselves swingers or swappers, and not nudists.

Be honest with yourself. If it's sex you're really after, please don't join a nudist group. Join a sex club instead. There are thousands of them out there, and we will all be much happier in the end.

Does Naturism Violate Christian Beliefs?

This chapter deals exclusively with the subject of naturism and Christianity, which is the nominal faith of the majority of our readers.
If you are a follower of another religion we can only apologise. It would be wrong of us to discuss nudism in respect of religions about which we know little or nothing, and we suggest that those of you who practice other faiths seek guidance from those who are qualified to give it.

A belief that the practice of nudism is incompatible with the teachings of the Christian faith causes much anguish and soul-searching in the hearts and minds of many of those committed Christians who are also attracted to the nudist lifestyle.

They have been taught that nudism runs contrary to Christian doctrine, and although they feel a deep affinity with naturism they are naturally unwilling to disobey what they believe to be a fundamental tenet of the Faith.

But just what is going on here? How can it be that a religion based upon gentleness and tolerance finds God's most beautiful and miraculous creation so abhorrent?

Clearly, something must be amiss, and we need to examine the Scriptures in a new light to discover just what The Bible and the Teachings of Jesus have to say about nudity.

We'd like to make clear at this point that we ourselves are far from qualified to make doctrinal judgements on such weighty matters, but fortunately we don't have to. Much study has already been done on the subject of Christianity and naturism, and there is a wealth of information, fully researched by frighteningly erudite intellectuals, to draw upon.

Most of this scholarly research is of such a volume that to reproduce it here would be both impractical and pointless. Should you care to study this subject in greater depth we have provided links in the resources chapter for you to use, but in this section we will limit ourselves to summarising, in brief, the opinion of the majority of those experts who have addressed this question.

Which is this.

Neither the Bible, nor the teachings of Jesus, indicate that Christianity is opposed to nudity or naturism, as practiced by nudists.

Far from it. There are many references to nakedness in the Bible, but it seems that The Almighty abhors nudity only when:

- It is forced upon a person against their will.
- It is associated with an act such as pagan worship.
- It means that the individual is lacking in basic needs such as shelter, food and clothing.

We can do no better than to quote this conclusion, found at *http://www.religioustolerance.org/nu_bibl.htm.*

'We have been unable to find a passage in the Bible that condemns public nudity, as in attendance at a naturist resort. There appear to be none that condemns private nudity. There seem to be a number of passages that mention nudity in the presence of others as acceptable behaviour. There also appears to be many instances in the history of the Christian Church where public nudity was a normal activity.
We would conclude that naturism is not disallowed by the Bible and that Christians should feel free to investigate naturism freely.'

Many nudists are also devout Christians, and find no conflict between naturism and their faith. Some worship naked, and find that being nude in nature brings them closer to their God. They point out that *'God made man and woman in His image, and they were naked'.* They also remind us that we too were born naked. How then can we consider the naked body to be shameful or obscene? As a devout friend says about nudity, 'If it's good enough for The Almighty, it's good enough for me!'

And perhaps, in the light of what you've just read, it will be good enough for you too.

If you're still not convinced, or you don't wholly trust the opinions of experts, here is what two very holy men had to say on the subject of nudity.

'His disciples said, "When will you be shown forth to us and when shall we behold you?" Jesus said, "When you strip naked without being ashamed, and take your garments and put them under your feet like little children and tread upon them, then [you] will see the child of the living. And you will not be afraid."

Gospel of Thomas-Saying 37

'Sexual modesty cannot then in any simple way be identified with the use of clothing nor shamelessness with the absence of clothing and total or partial nakedness. There are circumstances in which nakedness is not immodest... Nakedness as such is not to be equated with physical shamelessness. Immodesty is present only when nakedness plays a negative role with regard to the value of the person when its aim is to arouse concupiscence, as a result of which the person is put in the position of an object for enjoyment ... The human body is not in itself shameful, nor for the same reasons are sensual reactions, and human sensuality in general. Shamelessness (just like shame and modesty) is a function of the interior of a person.'

Pope John Paul II (Karol Cardinal Wojtyla)
Love & Responsibility, 1981

7

Naturism and the Law

Staying out of hot water

The situation regarding the legality of public naturism can be a complex and changing one, especially in the developing countries. Although we believe the following information to be correct at the time of writing, it is for guidance only, and does not constitute legal advice. As always, do your own research thoroughly.

Is naturism legal?

This is a big question, and the answer may vary according to the country you are in and where in that country you want to go naked. Also, remember that in a large federal republic like the USA the law regarding nudity varies from locality to locality and from state to state, and can even be interpreted differently by the various authorities at work within the same state.

However, the good news is that, in general, naturism is within the law in all western jurisdictions, including, but not limited to, those of the USA, Europe, Scandinavia, South Africa and Australasia, as long as it takes place on private land that cannot be overlooked by the public. This would include nudist clubs and resorts and possibly even your own garden.

Most of these countries also allow simple nudity at certain designated beaches, lakes, parks or watering holes, as long as you stay within the recognised limits and behave yourself. Some countries, such as Holland, are extremely liberal in their attitude to public nakedness, but even here there are some restrictions; a main shopping street, for instance, would probably not be considered a suitable place to stroll in the buff!

It's important to bear in mind though that things can and do change. A shift in the political climate, a swing in public opinion, a crusading politician or pressure from religious or political groups may easily force changes on long-held nudist freedoms, particularly at a local level, and as a result you may find, for instance, that a once official nudist beach is no longer sanctioned by the authorities.

The easiest and best way to stay inside the law is to seek out and join your national nudist association. As a rule of thumb you can assume that the existence of a national nudist association means that it is possible to practice naturism to some extent in that country, and, just as importantly, that there are like-minded people there with whom to share your interest. Furthermore you will be able to obtain up-to-date advice. If you are unsure of the legal position in respect of any nudist activity or location, it should be your first call.

Where nudity's a no-no.

Across large areas of the world social nudity is prohibited by religious, political or cultural strictures, and attempts at overt nudism—even whilst visiting or on vacation—may land you in very serious trouble indeed. The following is a very brief overview of the countries where going naked can get you into hot water, but it shouldn't be taken as definitive; there are over 190 sovereign countries in the world, each with its own laws and customs, and to attempt an exhaustive list would be impossible.

At the time of writing, naturism is forbidden in almost all of the Muslim countries such as Afghanistan, Iran, Iraq and Pakistan. Some nude beaches can be found in Turkey, but they are not officially sanctioned, and an attempt to open a naturist hotel there in 2010 sadly failed.

Nudism is not tolerated in many of the deeply religious, conservative Catholic countries of South America, although in Brazil, Chile and Uruguay it is allowed in authorised areas.

There are very few opportunities for naturism in Asia, except in Thailand, Indonesia, the Philippines and Israel. Japan has its traditional *Onsen,* or hot spring baths where mixed nude bathing can sometimes still be enjoyed, but is not otherwise particularly naturist friendly. The situation in China is confused; although state media insists that there is no law prohibiting nude swimming or sunbathing nude beaches rarely last long, usually due to government meddling or police harassment. Best not to attempt it.

There are strong rumours that South Korea might get its first nude beach by 2017. Apparently officials in Gangwon Province are aiming to set up a nude beach in an attempt to boost the country's east coast beaches, which lose out every year to the west coast in luring summer visitors from the capital Seoul. However there have been several false starts here in recent years, so keep an open mind on this one.

Africa, with the notable exception of South Africa, is, as far as we know, not sympathetic to naturism.

Our advice is to avoid nudist activities in any of these areas.

If you are wondering about the current legal status of a particular clothing-optional beach or location, you can try posting a question about it on one of the online nudist forums in addition to asking your national nudist federation.

To sum up then, if you intend to go nude anywhere in the western world, you will probably be within the law as long as you obey guidelines relevant to that country. Should you dare to go bare anywhere else, then be very careful, and expect the worst!

8

Naturism And The Single Man

If you are a single male interested in joining the naturist movement, we have to tell you right away that you may be in for a fairly rocky ride. It isn't going to be easy, certainly not the breeze it would be for a married couple or a single female.

For various reasons many single males feel that they are unwelcome, discriminated against or excluded from many nudist activities, especially within the UK. It is a situation that rightly infuriates them, but on the other hand the concerns of those who support such a seemingly unfair policy are to a large extent justified, or at least understandable.

However, don't despair. Being single and male no longer prevents you from indulging in the delights of nudism. Single men can and do gain membership of nudist clubs, and in any case private clubs aren't the only places to go nude. In a little while we'll be discussing ways and means for you to join in the fun, but first let's look at who nudists class as a *single male*. There are three types.

- The single male who is simply a man who currently has no female partner but would like to share his interest in naturism with other like-minded people.

- A married male whose female partner has no interest in or is hostile to naturism and has no intention of ever joining a nudist group. The male partner is still excluded even though he is married, as in order to qualify as a couple in many nudist venues *both* partners must join and attend on a regular basis and both are expected to be naked. (Although this may no longer always be the case.

See later in this chapter.) In many ways a man in this situation is in the worst possible position, because he has to contend with the disapproval of his partner as well as the perceived anti-single male bias of the naturist movement. More about this later.

> Be prepared for some double standards here. In many places a male will be accepted without his wife as long as another female accompanies him, whether or not she's his own wife. Few will question the nature of the relationship, or whether the wife approves—or even knows! Who says nudes are prudes!

• Men in gay relationships. Even in this day and age this bond is not universally recognised by traditional nudist clubs and the parties are regarded as two individual single males.

So why does the naturist movement have such a problem with single men?

The problem is this.

At any naturist gathering or event there will almost always be more—sometimes lots more—men than women. This is particularly true of locations such as free beaches, where it is difficult to monitor attendance. Only at those clubs or groups that are able to operate some sort of control system (by requiring a membership application for example), will there be anything approaching a balance between the sexes.

Nudist organisations will, for legal and public-relations reasons, rarely refuse to accept membership applications from single males. In practice, however they may enforce a deliberate balance system by limiting the numbers of single male members at any one time. New applicants are placed on a waiting list until one of the existing single male members drops out (or dies), at which point the next on the list is invited to join.

It is this 'quota' or waiting list system that causes so much resentment amongst single males. They point out that they are the only group of people who are treated this way. Male-female couples, families and single females are rarely refused immediate membership, unless they fail to meet the joining criteria in some other way, and they claim that they are being unfairly, and possibly illegally, discriminated against.

They have a point. However, the unpleasant truth is that without some sort of artificial restriction the resulting gender imbalance would threaten the very existence of many clubs and groups.

We're not being alarmist. This has already happened and we can give you a personal example.

Some years ago, a friend of ours who operates a large country house hotel decided to run a regular naturist evening in the hotel's sauna-suite every Friday night. Being an enlightened sort of chap, the only restriction he imposed was that attendees had to be BN (British Naturism) members. All were welcome, males, females, couples and families. If they could show proof of membership at the door they would be allowed in.

Delighted at the prospect of a new nudist venue on our doorstep, and anxious to support our friend in his brave new venture, we were only too happy to attend the opening night. Unfortunately though, we soon realised that Liz was the only woman amongst a crowd of some 25 men. Everywhere she went she felt 25 pairs of eyes on her. At first she pretended not to notice and got naked as normal. A little later she covered herself with a towel. Well before the night was over we were gone.

We never attended the Friday night sessions again.

Other married friends of ours did, and had much the same experience. They too stopped going. Eventually the Friday session became an all-male affair. Gradually the group, now unadorned by the fairer sex, began to lose its appeal and one by one the remaining men lost interest. Now, sadly, the Friday night sessions are no more.

Now, you might be wondering what the fuss was about. It was a nudist event. The ladies were nudists, and knew that everyone, including themselves, would be naked. So what was the problem?

Perhaps now would be a good time to correct a widely held but misguided notion about nudist ladies, and in doing so come a little closer to understanding why the gender imbalance causes so much dismay in mixed naturist circles.

It's a common belief, bordering on wishful thinking especially amongst textile males, that naturist ladies have no inhibitions when it comes to their own nudity and are happy to shed their clothes regardless of the circumstances. This is just not so. Nudist ladies are happy to be naked in public when it is comfortable and appropriate to be so, but resent any feeling of being put on show and feel just as vulnerable as their textile sisters when outnumbered by hordes of men.

In the same way, a husband or partner who would ordinarily have no problem with his wife or girlfriend being seen naked by others can begin to feel uncomfortable when a nudist event begins to feel more like a peep show—with his partner as the star!

The fact is that, with a few exceptions, even the most experienced lady naturists feel uncomfortably exposed when naked in an overwhelmingly male environment. If they find themselves in this situation, they will leave, and will not return. Consequently, fewer ladies will attend the next time and the imbalance becomes even greater, leading to still fewer ladies the next time and so on, until eventually the inevitable happens and the now all male club closes down due to lack of interest from the fair sex.

Which is why nudists organisations impose the quota systems that so frustrate and enrage single men.

The Root of the Problem

The root of the problem seems to be that, for reasons not really understood, far more men than women are drawn towards nudism in the first place.

Why should this be, and what, if anything, can be done about it? If, as many experts suspect, it's simply a case of genetic disposition then we'll just have to live with it, but maybe there are other factors at work here too.

The most widely quoted theory is that males are more comfortable with communal nudity because of the traditional male route through school, college, sports-club and the military, where shared shower and locker rooms are the norm. It's a plausible enough explanation but we just don't buy it. Many ladies now follow a similar path.

The next most popular hypothesis is that single men are drawn to naturism because of the unique voyeuristic and exhibitionist opportunities on offer. The reasoning is that males are naturally more inclined to admire the naked female body than vice-versa. The single male may have less of an opportunity to do this than someone with a partner. Nudism, with its unrivalled opportunities to get a free look at real life naked ladies, is therefore singularly attractive to the single-male.

There maybe an element of truth in this and some surveys have indicated that there is indeed a strong biological imperative at work here. However, the small numbers of men who may join for this reason can't account for the massive gender imbalance.

So, what is the real reason?

In our opinion

We don't accept that gentlemen are, by nature, any more inclined than women to naturism. The little research that has been done in this area indicates that when unencumbered by other pressures women are as ready to embrace naturism as their male counterparts. The real problem is that in the 'civilised' world the whole weight of social convention actively *discourages* ladies from dabbling with nudism.

Traditional wisdom has it that public nudity is improper, lewd and indecent—especially for women. Therefore any lady who willingly flaunts herself in this way must be immoral. Although intelligent people can see that this is absolute twaddle, many choose not to; these are deeply rooted beliefs, and are not easily overturned by rational thought. Furthermore, a lady who is attracted by the idea of naturism may first have to confront her own deep conditioning that nudity, particularly female nudity, is sinful, and for many this is the greatest challenge. (I speak from experience. See the next chapter.)

Ladies may also have a greater problem with their body-image, and have concerns about sexual harassment, exhibitionism and personal safety. And if this wasn't enough, they may worry about coping with the physical effects of their monthly cycle or pregnancy in a nudist environment.

All of these fears offer a huge disincentive to ladies tempted to experience the nudist way of life, and although they are to a large extent unfounded they have had a real impact on the gender split within the nudist movement. The imbalance is a serious problem, and, as we hope we've made clear, both sides have very real and valid concerns.

To sum up then, it's our view that:
* The gender imbalance is more a result of social pressures that *discourage females away* from the practice of

public nudity, rather than the *natural disposition of males towards it.*

- The quota system used by some organisations may discriminate against the single man and is possibly illegal in some countries. However, without it, many naturist groups and gatherings would simply become hopelessly gender imbalanced and eventually fail.
- A minority of males seek to join the nudist movement for its voyeuristic and exhibitionist opportunities. Whilst they are too few to affect the male-female balance in purely numerical terms, their activities may reinforce the uneasiness, fostered by cultural conditioning, with which nudism is viewed by many females.
- The single male is left feeling excluded from many aspects of naturism.

And now for the good news

So far we've painted a pretty bleak picture of the position of single men within the naturist movement, but don't lose heart. It's not all bad news. The law, and almost all of the national nudist organisations, are on your side.

These days, as we saw in chapter 4, there are many opportunities for you to practice naturism, even if you don't join a club. We'll take a closer look at some of these shortly, but first you need to make sure that you've done everything in your power on a personal level to increase your chances of acceptance into the naturist family. Below are some tips which will point you in the right direction.

Tip No 1. Join The Club

The very first thing you should do, if you haven't already done so, is to join your national nudist organisation. Every country in which social nudity is practised to any extent has one, and as far as we are aware they all accept applications from single males.

Membership of a national organisation will lend weight to your nudist credentials in three ways. It implies that you:

- Are a genuine inquirer after nudist enlightenment rather than a lightweight thrill-seeker and voyeur.
- Support the ongoing fight for a greater understanding and acceptance of nudism worldwide.
- Are who you say you are and have the willingness and ability to pay any membership fees.

Believe it or not, even such rudimentary vetting goes a long way in a movement such as ours. In fact some clubs and organisations will only consider applications from candidates who have been pre-screened via their membership of the national organisation.

Additionally, your organisation may furnish you with a register of clubs who are happy to accept single male members and also a listing of the saunas and swims in your area (see below).

Membership often includes subscription to the group's magazine, which is another good source of information.

Ironically, large numbers—perhaps the majority—of nudists world-wide don't belong to any national organisation, but we'd advise you to join as soon as possible. There is an annual membership fee, but it will be well worth it. It will serve you in good stead, and membership is highly recommended.

Besides, you'll have someone to complain to if you feel you're being discriminated against!

A guide to finding and contacting your national nudist association is given in the resources section at the end of this book.

Tip No 2. Bin the tin!

Do not turn up at your first—or preferably any—nudist event wearing nipple or genital piercings. They may look cool to you, but the wearing of body-jewellery is still a contentious issue within the nudist movement and many clubs and other organisations will bar anyone sporting them.

We realise this is a delicate issue with some piercees, who'll argue about civil liberties and personal choice. We even suspect that for some nudists the main reason for becoming a naturist in the first place is show off the piercing. However, this is not a forum for debating the rights and wrongs of piercing. You can hold whatever opinion you want, but the brutal truth is this; you won't offend anyone by *not* wearing genital jewellery, but you may well disqualify yourself from your preferred nudist group if you *do*, so why risk it? Life is hard enough for a single man trying to enter the nudist world as it is, so don't give yourself an additional handicap. Save the hardware for another time and place.

Tip No 3. Join in. Don't push in

If you are a stranger at a naturist gathering, particularly a mixed-sex event where most of your fellow nudists are with a partner, you might at first feel a little left out and marginalized, perhaps to the extent that you think you're being ignored. Don't read too much into this. It's not because people don't like you, but merely the natural reserve of any group of friends in front of a newcomer. It happens all the time, in most social situations, but because you are a single man in a mixed-sex nudist setting you might be more sensitive about it than normal.

The answer is not to panic, not to rush, and not to become resentful and rude. Obey the normal rules of etiquette. Be friendly, but not overly so, and don't be pushy. Don't intrude on private conversations, but don't be afraid to join in more open, general discussions. Above all, do not make lewd or suggestive comments, do not make references to your own or anyone else's body or say or do anything which could be misinterpreted or cause offence, especially in a mixed gathering and even if others are doing so. Remember that you are a guest, and a single man without a female. Your companions have allowed you to see their wives or girlfriends naked and they will expect you to act with respect, even if they allow a little risqué behaviour amongst themselves. If you don't, you will not be welcome.

Here's a real life example.

A little while ago we attended a sauna-swim evening at a nearby leisure centre. It was a privately organised affair, fairly small scale—about twelve couples—most of whom already knew each other. However, the organisers had invited along a single man, new to naturism, who had heard of the event via BN and had asked to attend. No problem so far. This is common practice.

During the evening we played a ball game in the bathing pool. Whilst jumping up to catch the ball, one of the ladies light-heartedly remarked how the movement caused her boobs to jiggle. This led to some mildly ribald banter which encouraged the other ladies to try the same thing, which, naturally, led to more slightly risqué chit-chat and laughter.

It was all very innocent, even childish really, but sadly, our unfortunate single male guest assumed from the tone of the conversation that it would be OK for him also to make personal observations about the ladies' breasts. It's a pity he hadn't read the advice in this book before he opened his mouth. He was not invited again, and has never been accepted into the nudist family. It may seem unfair, but that's the way it is.

Tip No 4. Keep trying! Get known! Be useful!

Familiarity doesn't always breed contempt. Go to your local free beaches and sauna and swims. Make yourself known. Gain a reputation for being friendly and helpful, but not a nuisance. In time you'll become accepted as a familiar face and you'll begin to make friends and be invited to other nudist events and clubs.

Here's an extra tip. If you have a trade or skill which is in great demand, such as expertise in building and landscaping or access to working vehicles or diggers, make sure that people know about it. Most landed clubs are always in need of someone like you, and we know of several single men who have had their membership fast-tracked because of their ability to plumb in a toilet, wield an expert chain-saw or provide an excavator at short notice.

Tip No 5. Just a little Respect!

Above all, wherever you are, respect the concerns of single ladies and married couples regarding single men. Don't stare, and don't stay dressed or hide yourself whilst others are naked, or you will be perceived as a Peeping Tom. Conversely, don't strut your stuff in an obvious way. It's considered to be exhibitionism, and it will work against you.

Where To Go Bare

We've already seen that there are thousands of places to get naked throughout the world. We're not going to discuss them in depth again, but lets see how 'single-male friendly' each category is.

Naturist beaches

Definitely the best places to go for your first taste of nudism, for the reasons we've already covered.

Sauna and swimming groups

These offer a good opportunity for the single male nudist.

The gender imbalance doesn't seem to be a significant problem here, and a quota system is rarely operated. If you hear of one of these groups in your area, we recommend that you get in touch with the organiser and ask for an invitation, making it clear you are a single man. You will seldom be refused.

Nudist vacations, resorts and centres

Not quite the open door to naturism that you would think, as some of the smallest centres and even some of the best known resorts may refuse bookings from single males, so check before you book.

The good news is that most of the larger resorts such as the huge Cap d'Agde complex in France have no such restrictions, and will welcome you aboard just so long as you can pay the bill. Be aware, though, that even the biggest centres may refuse to accept reservations from large parties of single men, so if you're going with friends, bear this in mind.

Internet and Special Interest Groups (SIGs)

The singles organisations and special interest groups that have sprung up on the internet are a good resource for the single male. Many of these have been founded especially for the single nudist and should be less concerned with the gender imbalance than other clubs. Be warned though (if it matters to you), that you may find yourself in an all-male environment.

Nudist dating agencies

The services of a nudist dating agency can be a good way to stop being a single male naturist and become a nudist with a nudist female partner. They can be quite expensive in purely monetary terms, but the outlay is more than compensated for by the saving in time and embarrassment. Remember that the lady you meet via this route is already a naturist, and is actively seeking a nudist partner. With your shared interest in nudism established from the outset you've no need to worry that weeks of careful and expensive wooing will end in a slapped face as soon as you suggest trying a naturist break somewhere.

Of course you'll still have to make her like you as a person, but that's your problem!

The Nudist Club

Ahh. . . The evil members' club. Those wicked organizations that exist purely to keep single men out of the nudist family.

A bit of an exaggeration perhaps, although if you've been on the wrong end of the quota system you may not think so. However although clubs may not be the easiest of the nudist organisations to break into, things aren't really that bad.

Remember that in many countries the law is on your side, making it an offence to discriminate against someone on grounds of gender. Whether you'd want to go to the trouble and expense of actually fighting your case through the courts is another matter, but in any case you will probably never need to.

Clubs, and the people who run them, are only too aware of their legal obligations and although it may sometimes seem that they comply with the law more in word than in deed, they will not want to push their luck too far.

Besides, although it may not be particularly obvious, single male members are actually valued quite highly. In member-owned clubs the members usually have to do nearly all of the maintenance work themselves. This is one of the more onerous responsibilities of being a member, and it is easy for members to 'forget' a work session, or be too busy to attend. Very often the single male member, who tends to be more willing and available for work and who can provide the muscle for the heavier tasks, fills the gap. And, as we mentioned earlier, if you are qualified to carry out one or more of the specialist jobs (eg. tree-felling, plumbing, fencing) or can provide useful material or equipment (a mechanical digger, chain-saws, building materials), you may well find that you are *invited* to become a member.

So, write to your national nudist association to see which clubs accept single members. When you've found one or more that are suitable apply directly to the club membership secretary. You might strike lucky and get accepted immediately. At the very least you should get on the waiting list. Don't forget; if you are able to travel, contact several clubs to maximise your chances of getting into at least one. (For more on this, see chapter 13, 'Taking The Plunge.')

Disapproving wives or partners

If you are a man with an urge to try nudism and a partner who hasn't, you have our sympathy. You have a double dilemma, as you have to face the hostility of your significant other as well as the barriers faced by other single males.

Unfortunately, the advice we can give you is limited, as it must be entirely a matter for your conscience alone whether or not you decide to walk the nudist way against her wishes.

With that in mind, here are our thoughts on the situation.

Firstly, and this isn't as stupid as it sounds, make sure that you have actually asked her.

During our time at Club Bon Ami we received many letters from married men seeking advice because their partners didn't share their interest in nudism. In a great number of cases we discovered that they had never even dared to suggest it! They assumed that their partner would disapprove, or worse, and they feared the effect on their relationship.

If this is the situation you are in, we'll give you the same advice that we gave them—just try asking, you might be pleasantly surprised. Remember that in nearly every case where a couple came together to try nudism, one partner had to be the first to put the idea forward.

The approach you take is up to you of course; she's your partner and you know best how to bring her round. (Heck, you persuaded her to join you in a relationship in the first place didn't you?) We would suggest however that you remember the points we made earlier regarding the way ladies are conditioned against public nudity, be considerate, and be prepared to give her plenty of time to think about it. It's a big step for her and if she'd been really keen on the idea she would have been the one to suggest it!

You may find that although she doesn't throw the idea (or you) out immediately she may need a little more convincing. Show her this book, especially chapter 9. You both may be pleasantly surprised.

When she agrees, remember that she, and presumably you, will be nervous newcomers. Your first experience is make-or-break time. Get it wrong and she'll never want to go socially naked again. But make it a wonderful, relaxing, uplifting experience, and you'll both be nudists forever.

Try a little compromise

If she still remains unwilling to take the plunge, try to find out the real reason. Is she against the whole idea of nudism generally? Or is it simply that she doesn't feel easy about getting naked in front of others? If it's the latter case, one compromise you might want to suggest is that you join and attend as a couple, but on the understanding that she can stay clothed until, if ever, she feels comfortable about getting undressed.

This is a situation which we have come across before, but it's not ideal and can be uncomfortable for all concerned. Until recently, most clubs would not allow such an arrangement, insisting that both partners should attend as nudists. However, new legislation indicates that such 'discrimination against an individual' is now probably illegal, and although at the time of writing (2015) the position isn't completely clear it's unlikely that any committee or club would dare refuse you membership on the basis of your partner refusing to get naked. It's certainly worth a try, and you never know—she might change her mind later on!

But if she still says no

If even this fails to move her, then you have no option but to respect her opinion. If you still feel the call, you'll have to attempt to persuade her to let you try it without her. Be honest about your intentions and attempt to obtain her consent, as most clubs, if they know you are married, will be unwilling to accept you unless they are convinced that you are applying with your partner's permission and knowledge.

Because of this some spouses lie about their marital status and declare themselves as single, but our advice is don't—it's not fair on anyone else and it always goes horribly wrong!

And if she prohibits you too?

Then you have a real problem and your options are limited.

You could secretly visit a nude beach or sauna-swim. Or you could employ a female escort who is willing to accompany you to a nudist area. Go ahead if your conscience allows and you think it's worth the risk. You might even feel so strongly about it that you are prepared to jeopardise your marriage by proceeding regardless of her feelings. It's really your decision and you're on your own with this one. Good luck!

Erections!

Although concerns about embarrassing erections are not confined to the single man, we include them here because the fear of an unwelcome physical reaction is a major worry for many men who are unaccustomed to being in the company of one or more naked ladies.

If this is something that bothers you, then relax. There is little to be concerned about. Nudity in a genuine, honest, naturist environment is not sexually arousing, so you need not fear that your natural instincts will embarrass you. We know you won't believe it until you've tried it yourself, but trust us. Don't let the worry of unpremeditated erections prevent you from experiencing nudism. It almost never happens.

Almost never. But it's not entirely unknown. So if you should find that your hormones are responding in an alarming way, do one or all, of the following:

- Cover yourself with a towel, or turnover onto your tummy.
- Take a dip in the cold pool, or ocean or whatever. If this is not possible, think about toothache or taxes to take your mind off it.
- Satisfy yourself that your fellow naturists (who may be causing your reaction) are also acting in a genuine naturist manner. If they are not, leave.

If the symptoms persist, as it says on the medicine bottle, examine your real reasons for becoming a naturist. Don't confuse naturism with exhibitionism, voyeurism, sex or pornography. If this is really what you want, admit it to yourself and join something more appropriate. You'll be much more comfortable in the end.

And now it's over to you.

We hope we've convinced you that it's entirely possible for an unattached single male to join the nudist family. We've done all we can. The rest is up to you. Keep trying. You *will* get there in the end. Don't give up.

Don't They Know That It's Different For Girls?

Naturism and Ladies

Ladies, this is the part where we lose the men for a while and talk amongst ourselves. Of course you can let the boys read this section later, but I think that it's important that we speak privately, girl-to-girl first. You see, as a lady nudist myself I think I understand the concerns and anxieties that you may be experiencing as you contemplate dipping a toe in nudist waters. I ought to—I've been through them all too!

(Forgive me if you're one of those brave and adventurous souls who can face the thought of shedding your clothes in a nudist situation for the first time without going into something of a decline. You are very fortunate. I have several friends who were able to slip into the nudist lifestyle without the slightest weakening of the knees, and I have always envied them their good fortune. If this sounds like you, you may want to miss this chapter and get started on some serious nude recreation right away. Don't wait for us. We'll catch up with you later.)

Unfortunately for most of us ladies, when it comes to thinking about going nudist things just aren't that easy. We females are subject to a unique set of cultural pressures, inherited preconceptions and social conditions that provide a powerful disincentive to those of us contemplating nudism. *Display our bodies? Why, nice girls don't, thank you very much, especially to complete strangers.* Sadly this mind-set is so deeply rooted in our collective psyche that the hardest struggle for most of us is to confront our own conditioning that nudity—especially female nudity—is immoral.

It's not an easy thing to do, and so I'm going to share with you the fears and feelings that I experienced when the subject of naturism first reared its head in our home. Hopefully you can identify with my personal anxieties at the time, and by learning how I came to terms with and eventually banished them completely you may do the same.

I've told my story from my own point of view, which is as a married women whose husband suggested naturism out of the blue. Your circumstances might be quite different; you might, for example, be an unattached lady with a hankering for the nudist way of life but experiencing some quite natural reservations. Whatever your situation, I hope that you will find something here to help and guide you.

My Story

Let me take you back to when I was a happily married young wife with two children, enjoying a quite conventional relationship with my husband. One evening we watched a now famous BBC television programme about nudists which caused a sensation at the time. I'm fairly sure it was called 'Let's Go Naked' but it was a long time ago, and the old brain cells have begun to creak a bit so I wouldn't bet the farm on it. ('Let's Go Naked' is now available on YouTube. If you want to see what all the fuss was about it's on our blog at *http://bit.ly/letsgonaked*)

Nowadays naturist documentaries are common enough, but back in the late 1970s the subject was taboo and this prime-time television broadcast provoked an uproar. It also generated a well-documented upsurge in interest in nudism, and one of those in whom it sparked curiosity—unbeknown to me at the time—was my husband.

A week or so after the programme he dropped the bombshell. I'd just put the children to bed and we'd settled down for a little time together. Out of the blue James produced a small pile of leaflets and booklets which, he explained, he'd received a few days before.

Well, you can guess what happened next. The publicity material was from the CCBN (now called BN, the British Naturist federation), and gradually, gently, Jim explained that he was attracted by the idea of naturism, and that he would like us to try it together.

I was outraged. I felt that the bottom had just fallen out of my world, and all sorts of negative emotions surfaced to torment me. I started to rant and rave, and cry and probably said some words that a well-bred country girl shouldn't even know.

To say that James was shocked at my reaction is an understatement. It was the exact opposite of what he'd expected.

You see, when we first met about seven years before, I was living in London, working in the antiques trade.

I was also moonlighting as a nude model.

I wasn't a nude model because I needed the extra money, although it came in handy. I became a nude model as the result of a challenge!

I'd never had a problem with the human body. I believed it was beautiful and sacred and something we should never be ashamed of. I thought nudity was natural. I had already enjoyed a little hippy skinny-dipping at a couple of rock festivals, I usually went bra-less, and I regularly wore the semi-transparent cheese-cloth garments that were fashionable then. None of this was particularly out of the ordinary at that time. It was just the way things were, a part of the liberal ambience which prevailed then. I loved that relaxed outlook on life, and never hid my feelings about nudity and the human form.

I suppose I must have championed these views a little too loudly and enthusiastically because when a friend of mine mentioned my name to a photographer who was looking for a nude model he did so as a challenge, to see if I would dare to stand by my principles. I admit I was a little shocked, and a bit annoyed, but couldn't really refuse if I wanted to retain my street cred.

So I took up the challenge, a little hesitantly at first, but I went on to enjoy nude modelling immensely and for a couple of years became quite in demand. I even had a nude part in an 'art' film, which was never completed. Maybe I'll tell you about it sometime.

I considered that what I was doing was art. I was celebrating the beauty of the human body, not debasing it. I refused to take part in some of the tacky exhibitions that passed for art in those days; I had very strict moral boundaries, and refused to go beyond them. It cost me a lot of work, I suppose, but I never compromised my principles.

When I met James I gave up modelling. He put no pressure on me. In fact we didn't even discuss it. It was my decision alone.

My feelings about the beauty and sanctity of the human body hadn't changed, and I still saw nothing wrong with nudity. But I also believed that as I had promised myself to James I should be nude for him alone. Nude in front of others was OK for single girls but not for a married woman. Although I would occasionally go discreetly topless on vacation in Europe, the rest of the time I mostly kept myself covered up except for when we were alone. It was an extension of my vow of fidelity. I guess I was still old fashioned like that.

Which was why I was so horrified at his suggestion. As far as I was concerned, public nudity was unthinkable for a married woman. To flaunt myself in this way would mean that I was a trollop, an immoral woman. We had willingly pledged to forsake all others, and now my husband was asking me to display myself naked to other men, which, now that I was married, was a form of unfaithfulness.

And as for nudists! I was disgusted. Everyone knew that nudists were deviants and sex-maniacs, and 'nudist colonies', as I thought of them then, were sordid places where revolting orgies took place.

Above all, I felt betrayed and humiliated. Foremost in my mind was the thought that my husband no longer loved me. I wasn't enough for him any more. He wanted to look at and lust after other naked women, and, as they were 'nudists' and therefore of questionable morals he would have no difficulty in finding compliant partners. If I allowed this, it would be the end of our relationship. For the first time in our marriage I felt sickened, frightened and insecure, and I believed I could never trust my husband again. I went wild. I told him I wanted nothing whatever to do with the idea. I shouted and called him names, and threw the CCBN stuff and told him where he could stick it. And then I ran up to bed and cried myself to sleep.

And if you tell me that my feelings didn't make sense I agree with you. The thing is, looking back on it, deep down even I, with my hippy agenda, was also associating nudity with sex.

Poor James! He had wanted a rational, civilised discussion, and I'd turned into a ranting mad woman who wouldn't even begin to listen to what he had to say. The next morning he apologised for suggesting the idea and promised that he would never, ever bring the subject up again.

Gradually the dust settled and things returned to normal—or at least as normal as they could. The damage had been done, and although I was happy to forget the episode, I didn't think I could ever forgive it.

And that's the way things would have remained, if it hadn't been for May.

Introducing May

May was a stalwart of our village, a churchwarden and everybody's favourite aunty. She and her husband of fifty-odd years Dennis—the local garage proprietor—were well into their seventies but still took an active part in the life of the community.

One spring morning May came round to sell raffle tickets for something or other and as usual she stayed for a cup of tea and to fuss over the kids. We got talking about our respective holiday plans and she mentioned that she and Dennis had booked to go to a newish resort in the south of France called Cap d'Agde.

Of course the name meant nothing to me then, but as we discussed the difficulty of deciding what clothes to pack for a ten-day holiday she dropped a bombshell.

'My dear,' she said, 'you should try our sort of holiday. We never wear clothes!'

Well, of course I was dumbfounded, and I spilled my tea down my blouse!

It transpired that May was a lifelong nudist, having been born into a naturist family. Her father, a prominent Scottish educationalist and her mother, a leading proponent of women's rights, were pioneers of the British nudist movement and had instilled in May the principles of freedom and equality— especially female equality— that underpinned their belief in the nudist philosophy.

Over the next few weeks we talked a lot about nudism. I'd told her about the row James and I had had and how the issues that it raised still hung like a cloud over our marriage. I guess it was more with the aim of healing my marital relationship than of converting me to nudism that she shared with me so much of her wisdom. In the end she did both, and a lot more besides, and for that I owe her my eternal thanks.

What follows is what I learned from her. I hope you find it as enlightening and as life-changing as I did.

How May taught me to look at my body in a new way

According to May, it isn't the naked female body that is obscene. It is the ingrained belief that female nudity is corrupting and evil that is the real obscenity. This was a notion that sprang from the male dominated early church, which was terrified of the influence of the female aspect of divinity that had held sway for thousands of years and always threatened resurgence. To counter the threat the church embarked upon a public-relations campaign that portrayed the archetypal woman as a temptress and a harlot, ever willing to use her body to bring about the ruin of man. Thus, female nudity became a symbol of wickedness, and two thousand years of female body-shame began.

Today, we see the result of this in the hypocritical (for which read *male*) legal stance on nudity that applies in many countries, including some of the more 'advanced' ones. Public displays of feminine nudity (nude or topless sunbathing for instance) are largely forbidden, but licensed strip clubs are OK. In other words, women may display their bodies only when permitted to do so by men, usually for the purpose of male enjoyment. Allowing women to get naked for their own enjoyment and well-being, at a time and place of their choosing, poses too much of a threat to public morality and is strictly prohibited.

This is unfair and demeaning to womankind. May believed that it's high time that women fought back, redressed the balance, reclaimed their rights and proclaimed themselves naked and unashamed.

Now, as you know, I personally had never felt that the human body was obscene in any way, but May helped me clarify my feelings and I was able to look at my body and naturism in a new light. With May's help I was able to think through my fears and prejudices and see them for what they really were, products of my social conditioning with no foundation in truth. Using this new logic I was able to dispel my greatest fears. As I thought for myself, instead of thinking the thoughts I had been taught to think, I began to see that nakedness doesn't have to mean sex, and being naked, even as a married woman, wasn't morally wrong. Suddenly naturism didn't look too bad. In fact, when I reflected upon May's teachings, it began to feel like my birthright.

The simple nudity practised by nudists is not immoral or obscene. We see it as immoral because that is how 'they' have wanted us to see it. Nudity, like money, is only immoral when it's used for immoral purposes. It is, after all, our most natural state. Innocent nudity is a wholesome celebration of the body that our God made for us, and to be ashamed of it is to be ashamed of His work. 'Think about it,' May used to say. 'God made you naked, so He obviously didn't think it was immoral. Who are you to disagree with Him?'

Being innocently naked in a true naturist situation is not the same as flaunting oneself, which implies putting on a provocative display for the sexual gratification of oneself and others. Such behaviour belongs in the bedroom, in private, not on the nudist beach. Genuine nudists, who retain their modesty, decorum and dignity even when unclothed, will not tolerate such behaviour.

May also made me realise how ridiculous was my generalisation that all nudists are perverts and wife-swappers. 'After all', she said, 'Who ever would want to swap with Dennis and me?' They were lovely people, but they were well stricken in years and suffered from arthritis and I could see her point!

It struck me that if the first—in fact, as far as I knew, the only—nudists I'd ever met were these two sweet and respectable old souls then there were probably a lot more like them and perhaps, after all, nudists were just normal people. Once we ourselves had become experienced nudists I discovered that this was indeed the case. The vast majority of nudists are morally upright and respectable, and although there are unfortunately a minority of so-called nudist groups who bring the movement into disrepute, they are easily recognised and avoided.

Well, of course, you know the outcome of the story. After my little talks with May, and to my husband's utter amazement, I asked to look again at the brochures, and agreed to try nudism for a limited time. Since then I've never stopped!

That was over 30 years ago, and during that time naturism has enhanced my life in so many ways that I can't imagine living without it.

Through nudism I've made wonderful friends, been to fabulous places and had some amazing adventures. I've enjoyed a supremely relaxing and healthy lifestyle, free of many of the stresses and constraints that beset most textile ladies. Most of all I am at ease with myself. I am self-assured, poised, and confident about my body and my femininity—whether clothed or naked. Every nudist lady that I know reports the same feeling of female empowerment, and it has to be the greatest gift that nudism bestows upon a girl. It can be yours for the asking too. Just come and get it!

Naturism and you

Just because your partner suggests that you try naturism together doesn't mean that your relationship is on the rocks, merely that he genuinely wants you to try a new experience together.

Let's face it, if all that he wanted was a bit of illicit nookie there's far easier ways to go about it and much more opportunity in the textile world. Nudity in a nudist situation is very non-provocative, nudist sites are far from being hot-beds of sexual intrigue and nudist ladies aren't all nymphomaniac babes, so if it's unbridled passion you're worried about forget the nudist club and watch out for the disco or even the office party!

Of course, some relationships do founder under the pressure of naturism. A fundamentally flawed relationship will rarely survive the questions of trust and understanding that nudism asks of each partner, and sooner or later the union will come apart and naturism will take the blame. But a fractured relationship will fall to pieces anyway; nudism may be just one of any number of reasons, but it's always the fragility of the actual relationship that is the underlying cause of the break-up.

By contrast, if there is any substance in your relationship at all, nudism will find it and build upon it. As you've seen from my experiences, naturism compels you to face issues such as love, trust, honesty and respect for each other and demands a critical appraisal of the bond between you. If you find strength and faith in each other then just go ahead and try naturism, because things will only get better. Your trust in each other will grow, and your commitment to each other will increase—and I can prove it. May and Dennis remained happily married for over 60 years, Jim and I have stayed happily hitched for 30 years so far, and—we may have been lucky, but this is the absolute truth—none, repeat none, of our many married nudist friends have ever got divorced. What other social activity can match that!

Phew! I've prattled on for far longer than I meant to, but I really wanted to help you confront some of the more serious issues with which you might be struggling as you consider indulging in nudism. I hope I've helped. Before I finish though, I'd like to briefly address the other, less emotional but equally worrying uncertainties that concern the potential lady nudist. (They certainly exercised my mind a bit.) I've put these in a question and answer form.

Answering your other concerns

But I'm too fat / thin / wrinkly / old'. Or My body is ugly / I've got surgical scars / bits missing.

These issues are the result of an inadequate body-image, and are extremely common, (especially amongst men, where one of the biggest concerns is the size of the 'equipment'). We've dealt with the subject of body-image at some length elsewhere, so I'll keep this short.

The plain fact is that just one visit to a nudist club or beach will dispel these anxieties for good. Nudists come in all shapes and sizes and some have bits missing altogether. (I've met a naturist lady who has undergone a mastectomy, and I know a nudist with a tin leg!)

One in every three nudists has surgical scars, probably less than 30 per cent have 'good' figures and maybe less than 10 per cent have perfect bodies. When you consider that the overwhelming majority of nudists are over 35 years old this isn't really surprising. So come on in, you look fine!

If you still find yourself expressing this particular concern, you may want to ask yourself if you're really:

- Using this as a convenient pretext to cover another, underlying reason for not wanting to try nudism. Be honest with yourself, and if you find that this is the case, identify and confront the real cause.
- Still mistaking nudity with sexual allure. There's nothing wrong with looking as attractive as possible, but remember that catching the eye of the opposite sex isn't

really the main aim of naturism. (Although if it is important to you, because, for instance, you're looking for a nudist partner, bear in mind that it won't happen at all until you get nude in the first place!)

I'm concerned about my safety, sexual harassment or exhibitionist behaviour, or that I'll be pestered by men.

There is really no cause for alarm. You are in no more danger in a nudist environment than you are walking the street —in fact, less so. Nudists are acutely aware that perverts may be drawn towards naturism in the hope of finding easy prey, and are constantly alert to the danger. Organised nudist sites and resorts are very well controlled and even most of the unregulated free beaches, where nudists are conscious of their often fragile legal status, are usually trouble free.

I have never experienced this problem myself, nor do I know anyone who has, and my advice is to take the normal, sensible precautions—such as not straying too far from the crowd—and just enjoy yourself!

I'll be embarrassed about my monthly cycle, or my pregnancy.

What is embarrassing about the fact that you are a normal woman? No one else will worry about these things.

When it's that time of the month do what the rest of us do— wear shorts or a bikini bottom. If you become pregnant, delight in the fact that your body is displaying signs of a new life and preparing for motherhood. It is a supreme celebration of your femininity, so please don't be embarrassed or ashamed. You'll find that every one will be overjoyed at your good fortune, so prepare to be spoiled.

Won't my husband find me less sexually attractive if he sees me naked too often?

No. Sexuality is in the mind and sexual attraction doesn't depend solely upon your partner seeing you nude—in fact seeing you in suggestive clothing will probably arouse him even more than it did before, so don't throw away those slinky dresses and revealing blouses just yet!

Why I should become a nudist anyway?'

Are you kidding? Read chapter 3, especially the section discussing the link between bra wearing and breast cancer, and you'll find twelve good reasons why. But that's not all. Because we ladies have three bonus incentives:

Bonus Reason #1

No white bits!

Bonus Reason #2

You'll find it so easy to make new girl-friends. At most nudist gatherings ladies are in the minority, which means that they tend to seek each other out and stick together. Striking up friendships is almost guaranteed.

Bonus Reason #3

Sometimes called *The Single Lady's Best Kept Secret*, it is the simple fact that there is an almost unlimited supply of eligible single men looking for romance in the nudist world— and nowhere near the competition you'll find anywhere else. If you are a girl looking for a date or a mate, take my word for it— you'll be spoiled for choice!

Think about it. 1.5 million ladies can't be wrong!

I'm glad we've had this chat, and I hope I've helped you with some of the issues that may have been bothering you. For more help and advice, please see the resources chapter.

Although precise figures are impossible to come by, we can make a very conservative estimate that some five million people worldwide practice naturism on a regular basis. We know that approximately 35 per cent of nudists are female, which means that almost one and a half million ladies have taken the plunge, and I'll guarantee that almost all of them experienced at least some of the concerns we've talked about. But they did it, and I did it.

And so can you.

10

Nudism, Partners and Relationships

Double the fun!

If you're in a relationship and you've both decided to find out a little more about nudism and its possible effect on your partnership, then this chapter is for you.

It would make our job very much easier if, at this point, we could provide you with some hard facts to prove that the practice of nudism is guaranteed to enhance your life together. It would be great to offer conclusive evidence that nudist couples suffer a much lower divorce rate than textile partnerships. Sadly we can do neither of these things. As hard as we've tried, and as much as we'd like to, we can find no genuine, verifiable data that *proves* that naturist marriages are happier, or longer lasting than non-naturist relationships.

You're just going to have to take our word for what follows—until you try it and find out for yourselves.

Nudism and your relationship

The simple truth is that empirical knowledge, as experienced by ourselves and others, indicates that if your relationship is in reasonable shape, and if you love, respect and trust each other—which is after all, what marriages should be about—then practicing nudism will almost certainly enhance your relationship and bring you closer together.

Well, we would say that wouldn't we? Nonetheless, it happens to be true, at least in our experience, which is considerable. We can truly assert that of the hundreds of nudist couples that we know well enough to vouch for, none have divorced or split up whilst actively practising naturism, a statistic that significantly beats the overall global estimates of 40/50 per cent of all marriages ending in divorce.

Now, even we don't claim that nudism is a panacea for the ills that beset every relationship or that two people need only to engage in nudism in order to guarantee a fairy-tale life together. Naturism alone will not resurrect a failed partnership nor will it heal a badly damaged one. (Although we know of a separated couple who independently took up naturism after the split and accidentally met each other at a nudist resort. The discovery of this hitherto unknown shared interest re-kindled the spark, and they've remained happily married—and nudists—ever since!)

But something is going on here, and the evidence overwhelmingly points to the fact that if you are a well-adjusted couple, who both willingly and voluntarily take up nudism together in a spirit of mutual love, respect and trust, then you are more likely by several orders of magnitude to enjoy a lasting and happy life together than most of the rest of the world—including those who start from an equally sound base but don't have the benefit of nudism to help them.

Why should this be so? Well, almost certainly because the underlying strength of the bond between you is reinforced by confronting the questions that nudism will ask of your partnership. Naturism will force you to examine your relationship, to hold it up to the light for inspection and to look candidly at the constituent parts, such as love, trust, respect and honesty.

What do we mean by this? Well, take for example the initial act of suggesting to your partner that you try naturism together. Let's not kid ourselves, asking a loved one to accompany you to a strange place where you will both strip naked in the company of total strangers is a pretty bizarre request, and your reasons for asking could easily be misconstrued. In order to even pose this question, you have to decide to trust your partner not to misunderstand your motive. Conversely, your partner has to decide whether or not to believe that you are acting in good faith. In this way, the issue of nudism obliges you to face up to truths about one another—in this case the question of trust— which most people would rather ignore, or prefer to take for granted.

Similarly, concerns such as jealousy, suspicion and possessiveness have to be confronted before you can be sure that nudism will benefit your relationship.

Nudism compels you to take a brutally honest look at your feelings towards one another. It acts as a magnifying glass through which you can examine those aspects of your relationship that many couples prefer not to look at too closely, Sometimes this critical appraisal isn't always easy or comfortable, but ultimately we believe it to be a worthwhile exercise for what it tells you about your real feelings for each other.

There is no doubt that a relationship has to have a sound foundation in order to survive the initial demands of nudism, and we believe that this, along with the fact that through nudism you will befriend other very happily partnered people, is the real reason why the vast majority of nudist partnerships are successful, happy and enduring. We are convinced that given a firm base, every relationship will gain enormous and long-lasting benefits from the practice of nudism.

Jealousy and possessiveness

Notwithstanding what we've just written, there is no doubt that concerns about jealousy and possessiveness do cross the minds of potential nudists, so we'll devote a little space to them here. If you've only ever been naked in front of each other, the question of what effect the presence of other naked people will have on you is bound to occur.

Generally speaking, nudity in a true nudist situation is non-sexual and non-arousing. Although there may be an initial shock when you get to meet your first nudist, this will soon wear off, and if you are expecting an instant turn on you're probably in for a mighty disappointment! Nudists are pretty matter-of-fact about the naked body, and neither display themselves provocatively nor leer at others in an offensive way. We'll guarantee that in a real nudist environment you will find very little to provoke the dreaded green-eyed-monster.

If you're a lady and you've ever visited a topless (top-free) beach with your husband you'll know exactly what we mean. Despite the presence of so many bare-breasted females, many of whom will be young, nubile and very attractive, there is no sense of sexual tension. For one thing it seems so natural; the setting calls for a minimum of clothing, and what might be erotic in another situation seems merely sensible on a beach. For another, when there are nearly naked girls in every direction even the most red-blooded male will eventually suffer from stimulatory overload and pick up a newspaper or take a nap!

Intimate relations

One of the concerns you may have as you contemplate trying out nudism together is that the practice will somehow adversely affect your sex-life, the assumption being that seeing one another naked more frequently will dampen your desire for each other.

This is, if you'll forgive us, total nonsense and is based on the old familiar falsehood that nudity equals sex. It's as ludicrous as suggesting that you turn into a slavering sex-fiend whenever you see your partner emerging from the shower or getting undressed for bed. (You do? Gosh! Either your partner is hotter than a fire cracker lit at both ends or you're reading the wrong book!)

As long as your relationship is secure, and founded on love and respect we can assure you that viewing your partner naked in a nudist situation, no matter how frequently, will have no adverse effect upon your sexual relationship whatsoever.

In fact, sometimes quite the opposite is true, and you may well find that, like some other couples, nudism gives your sex life a much needed boost.

There is a certain exhibitionist aspect involved in nudism that some people find stimulating, and in addition to the other benefits of naturism you may derive a mildly erotic thrill from the thought of displaying your partner naked to others. This reaction is not unknown and is fine as long as it remains a secret pleasure between you—a private game that is undetectable and offers no interference or offence to others. It has to be said though, that if it's your sole—or even your primary—reason for becoming nudists you would be better served by one of the many organisations that cater more specifically to your tastes.

'Till death us do part

It is a fact of life that death has the last word, and naturists are no more exempt from the laws of nature than any other group. Sooner or later even the happiest, most enduring relationship will end, with one partner being left to pick up the pieces of a shattered life.

When contemplating such a tragic event it seems churlish to consider what effect bereavement may have on your nudist activities, but there will come a time when the grieving is over and you will once again look towards your club for support and recreation.

Astonishing as it might appear, there are clubs that apply the policy that both partners must attend so rigidly that they will insist that the remaining partner, now no longer part of a relationship, must relinquish all current membership rights and re-apply as a single person This usually means taking a place at the back of the queue, which in the case of a male survivor is likely to be a long one. Fortunately, these clubs are in the minority and such callous behaviour is frowned upon. Most will offer unending sympathy and assistance and will be a source of enormous support at a difficult time, but it is an important caveat and something you should watch out for when selecting a club to join.

We've painted a pretty rosy picture of marriage amongst the nudists, but we're fully aware that there will be some couples out there whose experience of nudism has been just the opposite. Well, so be it, but we'd still argue that in those cases nudism wasn't the real cause of the problem. There must have been an underlying difficulty which nudism merely highlighted. We can only speak from our own experience, which is considerable, and our experience is that if your relationship is sound, naturism will make it stronger. Trust us on this.

Here's a few more tips before we move on:

- When considering nudism, you must engage in an open and honest dialogue. Don't try to hoodwink or browbeat one another; both of you must make the decision freely, or the whole thing will go disastrously wrong.
- Set yourself a trial period. Instead of making an open-ended commitment, which may appear to offer no turning back, why not promise one another that you will try nudism for six months, or ten sessions, or whatever? If one of you is particularly apprehensive, this will offer a get-out clause and may help to allay any feeling of being bullied into a situation from which it will be difficult to turn back.

- Should one of you decide to quit after the trial period, the other must stick to the agreement and respect the decision with good grace. Bullying, sulking or endlessly complaining about it is not only unfair but will do nothing for the relationship and will turn your partner against nudism still further. (Incidentally, for those of you who are already conjuring up a picture of this scenario based upon the assumed stereotypes, you might find the following fact instructive. According to our own totally unscientific but long running survey, in most nudist relationships it is the *male* who makes the first suggestion about trying nudism but it is the *lady* who is most keen to continue after the initial enthusiasm wanes.)

- If it doesn't work out because one of you isn't happy about getting naked in public you could try a compromise whereby the partner who is uneasy about nudity stays fully clothed. Although not popular with other nudists, clubs are under pressure to allow this situation. Refer back to chapter 8 for more about this.

- Never try to become a nudist without your partner's consent. It never works out!

- Don't tell anyone about your 'experiment' until you've made up your mind to continue. (If then.)

- And finally...'Doing it together doubles the pleasure!'

Nudism And Children

Children take to nudism like ducks to water, but how safe is the pond?

If you have young children, one of the uncertainties foremost in your mind as you contemplate a possible dip into nudist waters will doubtless concern the safety or otherwise of introducing the young ones to nudism at an early age.

The issue of children and nudism has become something of a cause célèbre amongst sections of the US establishment, and much has been made of the possible danger to young minds of an early exposure to adult nudity.

It is an emotive issue and one about which it is difficult—for the novice nudist parent at least—to obtain clear guidance. No other aspect of nudist culture is so emotionally charged, so hotly debated or is the subject of so many conflicting claims as the question of nudist minors, and in the face of so much uncertainty parents can be forgiven for playing it absolutely safe. No responsible parent will willingly put a child at risk, and many adults who are otherwise drawn to naturism will abandon the idea rather than expose a child to vague but terrifying dangers.

Which is a great shame. For, as we hope to show, verifiable evidence and the handful of academic studies that have been carried out on the subject indicate that family nudism is not only *not* harmful to a child, but its effects may be positively beneficial.

So why all the confusion and doubt?

A Brief History of Hysteria

The idea that children are damaged by an early exposure to nudism was popularised by such prominent gurus as Dr Benjamin Spock and Dr. Joyce Brothers, whose opinions were, and still are, hugely influential in shaping attitudes towards childhood development. Indeed, these two were considered so academically irreproachable that most subsequent observers accepted their findings unquestioningly and passed on their ideas without ever conducting any new research of their own.

It was a message that struck a chord with the early anti-nudist campaigners and added more force to their argument. Not only was nudism wrong, but respected academics agreed that forcing (as they saw it) children into nudism was *horribly* wrong. Armed with this new weapon they renewed their attacks upon the nudist movement with increased vigour.

Despite the vitriolic nature of the argument it remained an issue of only passing interest to the majority of the population and it's unlikely that the row would ever have entered the mainstream of national debate if it wasn't for two emerging trends; the alarming rise in reported paedophile crimes across the western world and the swing to the right of many American institutions.

With the convergence of these two phenomena the issue of children in nudism became hot news and a matter for widespread public concern. Powerful voices began to argue that family nudism, already perceived by much of the establishment as a perverse pursuit, was an ideal environment for paedophile activity. By thrusting their children into naturism, parents were placing their children in harm's way—sometimes, it was hinted, deliberately. Not only was nudism emotionally harmful to children but it also placed them into direct contact with the paedophiles and perverts who, as every right thinking person thought they knew, prowled nudist areas in packs, just waiting for an opportunity to pounce.

It was a disturbing picture that roused the indignation and wrath of much of the Great American Public who, being largely unacquainted with the real nature of genuine nudism and without access to any evidence to the contrary, swallowed the whole story, red-herrings and all.

The impetus continued and the process has now become a political juggernaut that has inevitably and rapidly attracted its full complement of band-wagon-jumpers and vested interests.

It is, after all, an opportunity too good to miss. Nudism is already a widely misunderstood and suspect activity, particularly in conservative America, and this new dimension has made it an even more attractive target to go after. Anti-nudist activists who had previously failed to find any rational objection to nudism in itself have breathed a sigh of relief at finding at last a seemingly genuine reason for their opposition. Political opportunists, some of whose own backgrounds don't bear close scrutiny, have eagerly capitalised on popular sentiment and made exaggerated claims of their own. And even some commercial interests have made a quick buck by using the 'nude minor' objection to overturn planning permission already granted to nudist developments in order to obtain the land for their own profit.

In short, what started as a spat between two minority groups with opposing but genuinely held views has become a circus into whose ring anyone with an agenda can throw their hat. Hysteria has taken the place of reason. Confusion has supplanted clarity. We find obfuscation where we seek information. And things don't seem to be getting any easier.

There is now in a situation in the USA where nearly every nudist activity or application is routinely challenged. Many beaches are under threat. There is an influential lobby in favour of outlawing nudist youth camps altogether and proposed legislation banning family social nudity on the basis that the 'offending' adult may be '*grooming the child to be more receptive to sexual abuse in the home.*'

According one prominent observer, the U.S. National District Attorney's Association is now saying that a potential child molester can be identified as one who '*aims to get the child comfortable seeing nudity.*'

At this point you may be forgiven for wondering just who should be accusing whom of becoming obsessed with naked children!

It's no wonder that in some parts of the USA many decent, responsible naturist parents are frightened to admit that they are nudists for fear of ridicule, exclusion or even prosecution.

But just how real are the accusations aimed at the nudist movement?

The Naked Truth

Let's try and cut through the hype and hysteria and take a more balanced view of the situation. In essence, the two main concerns regarding children and naturism are that:

- Being raised in a nudist environment with nudist parents will have a negative effect on the personality of a young child, leading at best to a guilt complex, social problems and sexual obsessions, and at worst to incest and abuse.
- Children will become unacceptably vulnerable to the paedophiles who, it is assumed, infest nudist areas and events in droves.

We'll examine each of these situations objectively, using both empirical data and the small amount of academic research that has been carried out on the subject.

Concern 1: The risk of social and emotional damage

The assertion that a whole range of children's problems can be blamed on an early exposure to nudity around the home would, if it were proved to be true, be enough to lead any responsible parent to put a double lock on the bathroom door and renounce the nudist idea for good, or at least until the kids had grown up and flown the nest.

But what is the experience of ourselves and others who have already brought up children within a nudist environment?

The Light of Experience

Fortunately, those of us who took up naturism in less P C days never realised that we were putting our offspring at so much risk, poor, naive innocents that we were. We blithely carried on, exposing our children to the horrors of a healthy attitude to the human body and the wholesome happy atmosphere of a family nudist club. Luckily our children didn't recognise the danger they were in either, and grew up to be the normal, well-balanced adults who are even now introducing their own children to naturism.

Were we just lucky? Or do we know something that the (invariably non-nudist) experts don't? Because, let's be honest here, if you believe that there is any justification in the prevailing sentiment that children are put at risk from nudism then you are accepting that many thousands of caring nudist parents with young children are deliberately and wilfully placing their offspring in danger of serious long-term emotional damage.

It is a serious charge. It's also nonsense.

Nudity is a natural state for children, as any mother who has watched her child gleefully scamper around in the buff will confirm. It is only when we teach them that being naked is wrong that they pick up feelings of shame, guilt and embarrassment about the human body.

Children brought up in a nudist environment *are* different from more conventionally raised children, agreed, but not in the way that the anti-nudist legislators would have us believe. Because, far from being emotionally blighted, nudist children obtain and retain a more rounded view of life, greater self-esteem and suffer from less hang-ups than non-nudist children, and the overall effect makes a positive difference to their whole life.

However, there is an important caveat. It's our belief that *this is true only if children are introduced to naturism at birth, or at very early age, when attitudes and prejudices have not yet been shaped by the world around them.* Trying to introduce older children—nine-year-olds for instance, who are already grappling with the insecurities of life and who are starting to form their own world-view—to nudism can have a detrimental effect and in our opinion should be avoided. We've more to say about this later in this chapter.

As a rule even children raised in a naturist family from birth grow less interested in naturism with the onset of puberty, when the combined effects of hormonal imbalances, other interests, and the fact that most of their friends and members of the opposite sex are to be found outside the naturist environment, make nudism hopelessly 'uncool'. But although some older children abandon naturism for good, many others return as young adults to introduce new partners and their own children. Surely these are hardly the actions of people whose lives have been damaged by nudism?

All this is, of course, exactly what you'd expect us to say, but it's nonetheless true. We are talking with the benefit of some 30 years experience of naturism, which is approximately three decades more than any of the scaremongers, few, if any, of whom have any familiarity with real naturism.

We have seen our own and other children grow up in a nudist environment without any problems and some significant benefits, and we are now seeing a brand new generation being brought into the same fold. It is our honest opinion that as long as the child is part of a normal happy, caring and supportive family, and naturism is kept within the bounds of normality, for instance not forced, exaggerated or emphasised to an unhealthy degree (we've more to say about this later in this chapter), then your child will suffer no emotional damage and will very likely benefit from the experience.

These are our feelings based upon our own knowledge and experience, and although they are genuinely and firmly held you might understandably consider them to be biased. So let's leave the realms of practical experience and take a more scientific approach.

Academic Research

Unfortunately little theoretical and less practical research has been done on the nature of nudism as a whole, and the subject of children in nudism has received even less attention.

The small amount work that has been done on naturism has tended to be part of a wider investigation into sexual habits and conventions. (Reflecting, infuriatingly, the continuing association between nudity and sex made even by those who should know better.) Fearing that the inclusion of children into any such research would be an unacceptable breach of decency, most investigators ignored the issue altogether, leaving us with the present scarcity of information.

With so little in the way of new academic evidence becoming available, campaigners have been forced to fall back upon the little research that had already been done, most notably, and most prominently, the findings of Spock, Brothers, et al., who, as we have seen, promoted the view that nudity was damaging to children.

As these were the leading lights of the child psychology field at the time, their opinions were generally accepted unconditionally, and for many years no one thought to query the soundness of the research.

Recently, however, some observers have questioned the validity of Spock's findings, contending that his conclusion was not the result of scientific study but was based upon one anecdotal incident involving his own son.

Similarly they caution that Dr. Joyce Brothers, who warns parents of the 'terrible guilt and frustrations' that children suffer from being exposed to normal nudity, seems not to have performed any research of her own but apparently based her conclusions on her work with emotionally disturbed children.

Now we ourselves are not able to prove or disprove these statements, but they do raise an interesting question. If we accept that a widely held public perception can be based upon nothing more than anecdotal evidence, then we must accept that anecdotal evidence to the contrary must be equally valid. And such evidence abounds, not only in the experiences of thousands of ordinary naturists like ourselves, but also in the opinions of other respected researchers.

For example, Dr. Lee Salk has said:

'Being natural and matter-of-fact about nudity prevents your children from developing an attitude of shame or disgust about the human body. If parents are very secretive about their bodies and go to great lengths to prevent their children from ever seeing a buttock or breast, children will wonder what is so unusual, and even alarming, about human nudity.'

Dr. Lloyd de Mause, Director of the New York Center for Psychoanalytic Training, observed:

'There is no evidence supporting claims that exposure to nudity produces a higher number of psycho sexual problems in either children or adults who were raised in such an environment.'

And Ted Polhemus wrote:

'Writing as someone who has visited several naturists resorts, it seems to me that the basic tenet of the naturist/nudist movement—that prurience can be diminished by the innocent exposure of the body—has been proven correct. One sees this most clearly in the children of naturists who have grown up in an environment which is free of the sniggering innuendo of the tabloids.'

Researchers Dennis Craig Smith and William Sparks spent over five years (plus added years for follow-up on some cases) investigating the experiences of adults who had been brought up in an open physical environment. Their seminal work, snappily entitled *'The Naked Child Growing Up Without Shame/Social Nudity/Its Effect on Children'* documents their findings and concludes that children's exposure to social nudity, far from being harmful, is generally beneficial.

A document filed by British Naturism with the Scottish government in 2009 claims that children brought up in countries where nudism is more freely practised were less likely to suffer unwanted pregnancies during their teenage years than those from less nudist friendly countries. A spokesman for British Naturism is quoted by The Daily Mail as saying *'There is strong evidence that conventional attitudes towards the human body contribute significantly to a wide range of problems, some of them serious—but there is incredible reluctance to face the implications.'*

We could continue quoting sources and evidence *ad nauseum*, but it would serve no useful purpose. Much more information is available on the internet for anybody wishing to make a comprehensive study of the subject, and a list of possible sources is given in the resources section of this book. However, for our purposes the small sample shown here is adequate to make the point that although the negative findings of Spock and company are still held in tremendous esteem, there is equally as much, if not more, evidence pointing to the fact that children are not at risk of psychological damage from nudism.

Before we move on, we'd like to share one more thought with you.

Despite a host of equally credible findings to the contrary, much is still made of the original conclusions reached by Dr Spock. However, Dr Spock's work was originally published in 1946, which means that two generations of nudist children have already grown to adulthood under the burden of a naturist childhood.

According to Spock's theory, many thousands of individuals whose minds have been damaged by nudism have been introduced into society over the past 60 years. And yet we can find no record of any case where criminal behaviour has been attributed to a nudist childhood!

Clearly something doesn't add up.

Concern 2: The danger from paedophiles

Unlike the largely illusory perils examined in the previous section, the threat to our children's well-being presented by paedophile activity is, unfortunately, a very real one.

Sadly the paedophile menace contaminates the nudist movement just as it infects every other facet of modern life in which children play a part, and the fact that we are no more a focus for its attentions than, say, the school gate or public swimming baths gives us no comfort.

Unfortunately, we also feel compelled to say that in our view the nudist movement generally has been unforgivably slow to react to this danger.

As we mention elsewhere in this book, vetting procedures are often rudimentary and sometimes woefully inadequate—a situation that we personally have campaigned to address—and occasionally, very occasionally, one of these creatures has slipped through the net, avoided the watchful eyes of the other members, and struck. The dangers of complacency were highlighted when it was discovered that one well-known naturist, still widely quoted by nudist web sites for 'proving' that nudity is good for children, has himself been prosecuted for crimes against minors. Whilst this may not negate his findings it certainly leads one to question his impartiality and proves, if proof were needed, that we must never relax our guard against these sub-humans.

So does this mean that the nudist movement should be banned, that nudist resorts and beaches should be closed or that parents with young children should stay away altogether?

No, most definitely not. Because when viewed in its proper perspective, and approached with common sense, the problem comes down to a manageable size.

But just what is its proper perspective?

Unfortunately, this is another issue about which it is difficult to garner relevant statistics. Although individual cases are well documented, and, of course, widely and eagerly reported in the press, exhaustive research has failed to uncover any mention of naturism itself as being a cause of or a focus for paedophile activity. We have been unable to find, for instance, any record of the proportion of paedophile crime committed by persons who have been engaged, however marginally, with organised nudism, nor is it possible to obtain any overall comparisons between offences committed on or at nudist locations or events and those committed at non-nudist occasions.

If nudism was considered to be a major, or even significant, trigger for paedophile activity, we can be sure that the fact would appear in at least one of the many papers that have been published on the subject over the years. Yet, as far as we have been able to establish, it does not. Perhaps then, in the absence of any specific finger pointing, we are justified in reaching the conclusion that the nudist movement is neither perceived nor shown to present a greater than average threat to children from paedophile activity.

We agree that making a deduction based upon what *has not* been reported rather than what *has* is not the most satisfactory or scientific method of reaching a meaningful conclusion. Unfortunately, though, it is the only method available to us and does at least fit with the facts as experienced by ourselves and other veteran nudists, namely that paedophile activity in the nudist environment is extremely rare—we personally have never come across a case, nor have we met anyone who has—but, sadly, not unknown.

However, nudists are acutely aware that the environment from which they gain so much innocent enjoyment is also attractive to others with far more sinister motives, and therein lies our best line of defence; we are acutely alert to the danger and on guard.

The majority of nudist membership clubs tend to be small-scale affairs, mini-communities where everybody knows everybody else and watches out for each other. Such an environment offers little opportunity for the paedophile or any other dodgy character to cause trouble, as any form of aberrant behaviour is easily and quickly spotted and the offender is shown the gate before any damage is done. Thankfully, paedophiles find it difficult to operate under these conditions.

There is a much greater potential for danger on the nude beaches or gigantic holiday complexes, however, where the combination of unregulated attendance, large numbers of people and lack of a community atmosphere makes it almost impossible to guard against paedophile infiltration.

These factors also contribute to another menace; the scourge of the secret camera. Now that miniature cameras and ultra-long lenses are widely available it's easy for a paedophile to photograph children (or adults), on a nudist beach and share or sell the photographs over the internet that same day. The fact that the children aren't physically assaulted doesn't minimise the despicable nature of the act nor the potential for danger.

So, we agree that there is a real problem, but although we must not ignore or underrate the threat, neither should we overstate it nor let it spoil our chosen way of life. Other, better known and highly regarded institutions and environments have proved to be far more vulnerable to paedophile attack and yet, rather than capitulating to the menace and shutting up shop they are actually growing exponentially. (The internet itself for instance. According to the Internet World Stats website *http://www.internetworldstats.com/stats.htm* worldwide internet usage in 2014 has grown by *741 per cent* since the year 2000 despite warnings from Crimes Against Children Research Center at the University of New Hampshire that one out of seven children will receive an unwanted sexual solicitation whilst online.

The nudist movement can and should do more to guard against these monsters in our midst, but until we get our house completely in order nudist parents should recognise that nudism places a child under no greater threat than many other activities, including surfing the 'net at home. Forewarned is forearmed, and where a threat does exist it can be diminished by practising proper parenting, closely supervising your child at all times and taking sensible precautions, just as you would anywhere else.

Conclusions

The evidence, both empirical and academic, points to the fact that exposure to nudism, if carried out in a loving, caring family environment is not psychologically or emotionally damaging to children and in fact seems to be positively beneficial. Children who are raised as nudists, or in nude-friendly families, grow up to be adults who are comfortable with their bodies and their sexuality.

Whilst the threat of paedophile activity is very real and should not be minimised, actual instances of offences by nudists, or within a nudist environment, are rare, much more so than in some better regarded institutions and environments.

Therefore we see no reason for parents of young children to avoid the pleasures of family naturism as long as they are aware of the potential for danger and take all sensible precautions.

In other words, be aware, take care, but don't throw baby out with the bathwater!

Just before we move on, here's a few more tips.

- Don't make a big thing about nudity. When it occurs it should feel entirely natural, gentle, and comfortable and not become the subject of debate or drama. Avoid artificial, embarrassing, uncomfortable or over-emphasised situations, like insisting on routine nudity around the home. Above all, never insist that the child goes naked when he or she doesn't want to. Being nude should be like owning a goldfish, a totally unremarkable, minor but entirely natural part of normal life.

- Children are safer in a club environment, but check that the club is suitable for family membership before you join. Although most clubs try to be honest about their ambience, 'family friendly' can mean different things to different people. Even genuine clubs may stage things like lingerie shows, nude beauty pageants and risqué fancy dress nights that may make them unsuitable for families, so know before you go!

- Explaining to an older child that you are contemplating nudism can be very difficult. Many of his or her perceptions, including the familiar body-taboos, have already been formed. To avoid unpleasantness and embarrassment you may prefer not to tell pubescent siblings about this aspect of your life at all, restricting your nudist activities to school times etc. when the child is being looked after by another adult. It may seem a little dishonest and bit of a hassle, but it's probably the best course, and many of our friends and acquaintances have successfully chosen this path.

- If you have children by a former marriage who you want to bring to a nudist club, be aware that for legal reasons clubs are increasingly insisting on written consent from the other natural parent before they'll allow the children to attend.

- **Above all, always remember The Golden Rule. The well-being, safety and happiness of our children is our absolute number one overriding priority. Their welfare must always come first.**

Nude Health

Are you exposing yourself to danger?

Despite being nudists for more years than we care to remember, we are unable to think of a single health concern to which nudists are uniquely susceptible. Whilst it's true that the practice of naturism outdoors may involve some minor risks to one's well-being, these are hazards faced by everyone who spends time in the open air, and are not exclusive to naturists.

If you've read chapter 3 'Twelve Good Reasons To Become A Nudist', you'll realise that much of the following section regarding the danger of exposure to the sun conflicts with the latest research which indicates that it's safer to expose yourself to too much sun than too little. Confusing, we know, but we have to bring you all the evidence. In the end, your own common sense must be your guide.

Let's examine the hazards you may face.

Dangers from the sun

Melanoma

This is undoubtedly the cause of most concern to nudists, and with good reason. Every year in the UK alone over 40 thousand people get skin cancer and 1500 die from the most serious form, malignant melanoma.

Melanomas are usually caused by DNA damage resulting from exposure to ultraviolet (UV) light from the sun, although it is thought that genetics also play a role.

Other sun-related dangers are:

Premature ageing of the skin (Photoaging)

Chronic exposure to the sun causes changes in the skin called actinic, or solar, degeneration. The skin over time becomes thick, wrinkled, and leathery. This condition has often been referred to as *premature ageing* of the skin. Since it occurs gradually, often manifesting itself only after many years of exposure to the sun, photoaging is often regarded as an unavoidable condition, a normal part of growing older. With proper protection from UV radiation, however, photoaging can be substantially avoided.

Cataracts

Cataracts are a form of eye damage, a loss of transparency in the lens that clouds vision. Left untreated, cataracts can rob people of sight. Research has shown that UV radiation increases the likelihood of certain cataracts. Although curable with modern eye surgery, cataracts diminish the eyesight of millions of people worldwide, and necessitate millions of dollars of eye surgery each year.

So how real are these dangers?

The idea that nudists are more prone to skin cancer and other sun damage because of their total nudity just isn't really true. The modern bathing suit covers just a few square inches of the body, and in any case doesn't provide any protection against the sun's harmful UV rays.

This is born out by medical evidence. Melanomas most frequently occur on the upper backs of both sexes and the legs of women, but can actually occur anywhere on the body. If nudism increased one's chances of getting skin cancer, one would expect to find a wider incidence at those areas that only nudists expose —the nipples and genitals.

Besides, contrary to popular opinion, nudism isn't just about getting an all-over tan. Many nudists, ourselves included, avoid the very hot sun, preferring the shade of the trees during the warmest part of the day. Nudism is a total experience, an opening up of the body to the elements, a gently fulfilling experience that does not include exposure to extremes of either heat or cold. As we've already mentioned, one of our own favourite nudist activities is to walk naked through silent woods in good company.

But back to the sun. Although nudists aren't at any greater risk from the sun than textile bathers, they are fully aware of the dangers and most take them seriously. You'll find that nudists observe the same common sense precautions as anyone else, and if you follow the following guidelines you should avoid any major problems.

- **Avoid the sun completely if possible between 11am and 3pm**. If you happen to be on holiday somewhere hot, this is a great time to find a cool bar or restaurant for some midday refreshment, or to retire to your room for a siesta.

- **Wear a hat!** Yep, We've seen many otherwise naked people wearing hats. Wide-brimmed is better than baseball style. And we've also seen any combination of long sleeved tee-shirts, scarves, dresses and jogging bottoms too, when necessary. We're nudists, not nuts, so don't be afraid to cover up if you need to. You can always undress again when it's safe to do so.

- **Take advantage of sun-shades,** but don't rely exclusively on one for protection. Water, sand and concrete all reflect a high proportion of UV light. UV also penetrates glass, cloud, water and fine fabrics, so many so-called sun-shades are of little more than ornamental value.

- **Slap on the cream.** Generously apply about one ounce of sunscreen to cover all exposed skin 15 minutes before going outside. Sunscreen should have a Sun Protection Factor (SPF) of at least 30 and provide *broad-spectrum* protection from both ultraviolet A (UVA) and ultraviolet B (UVB) rays. It should state that it's *broad spectrum* on the label. Re-apply every two hours, even on cloudy days, and always after swimming or sweating.

  Pay special attention to the sensitive areas like the nose, ears, eyelids, soles of the feet, lips and, if the hair is thinning and you haven't got a hat, the top of the head. And, especially when naked, be careful to protect the nipples and genitals.

  Re-apply your sun screen frequently (at least every two-three hours) or whenever you towel off, otherwise your protection will be reduced.

  Infants under six months of age should be kept out of the hot sun altogether. Their skin is too sensitive for sunscreen.

- **Always wear good quality sunglasses.** OK, you probably do anyway because it makes you look cool (go on, admit it), but you should always choose those that block 99-100 per cent of UV radiation, as this level of protection will greatly reduce the sun-exposure that can lead to cataracts and other eye damage. Some manufacturers' labels may claim *UV absorption up to 400nm,* which is the same thing as 100 percent UV absorption. Wraparounds are the best. Sunglasses that wrap around the temples prevent the sun's rays from entering from the sides. Some studies have shown that enough UV rays enter around standard sunglasses frames to reduce the protective benefits of the lenses.

One other thing about sunglasses. There is a theory that shading your eyes from the sun for a long period can actually *increase your chance of burning*. The reasoning is that the body takes much of it's information regarding sunlight from the eyes, and that by artificially darkening them for long periods you fool the body into thinking that the sun is less strong than it actually is. This in turn inhibits the production of melanin, the body's natural tanning pigment that protects against UV rays, making burning more likely. To prevent this happening, remove your glasses for two or three minutes every fifteen or twenty minutes or so.

- **Avoid sunlamps and tanning salons**. Sun beds damage the skin and unprotected eyes and are best avoided entirely. This is so important that we'll repeat it. *Avoid sunlamps and tanning salons. Sun beds damage the skin and unprotected eyes and are best avoided entirely.*

- **Check out the danger from the sun's ultraviolet rays where you are.** Go to the UV Awareness site at *http://www.uvawareness.com/*, and type your location into the search box to quickly check out the possible danger from UV radiation in your area. The site also gives recommendations regarding the suggested level of protection you should take. The information is updated hourly.

  The site uses the UV Index, which was developed by the World Health Organisation in collaboration with the United Nations Environment Programme, the World Meteorological Organisation, and other bodies. The UV Index is a scale ranging from 1 to 11+. It describes the level of solar UV radiation at the earth's surface at any given time and is an indicator of the potential for associated health risks. It also takes into account clouds, altitude and other local conditions that affect the amount of UV radiation reaching the ground in different parts of the world. It's a great aid to helping you plan your outdoor activities in ways that prevent overexposure to the sun's rays.

When the index is High or Very High, try to minimize your outdoor activities between the peak hours of 10:00 am and 4:00 pm when the sun is most intense. When the index is 10 or higher, stay indoors if possible, otherwise be sure to take all the other necessary precautions.

Before we leave the subject of tanning, here's a thought for those of you who think that a deep dark tan is a big turn-on for the opposite sex.

According to a survey by Bergasol, the French sun-cream makers, 69 per cent of men and 51 per cent of women find a light tan more attractive than either a dark tan or no tan at all. Only 15 per cent of men and 20 per cent of women find a dark tan attractive, and 75 per cent of men and 59 per cent of women consider women with a light tan more sociable than women with a dark tan or no tan at all.

So before you're tempted to sizzle for just one more hour, take heed!

Dangers from insects and other creepy crawlies

In general these affect nudists no more than they affect the rest of the population, and the same precautions should be taken.

- Wasp and bee-stings may be a little more painful and embarrassing if they occur on less usual parts of the body, especially if you are one of those unfortunates who need medical treatment after a sting, but a little common sense and insect repellent should prevent this in the first place.

- Always wear footwear when walking, even on grass or sand. Ants and sand-flies can bite, and anyway the soles of the feet are the most tender part of the body.

Danger from Accidents

Accidents can happen anywhere, and although we can think of none which are unique to naturism there are some issues relating to nudism and accidents that we should explore.

Life on a nudist site can be very lively. As well as enjoying the usual games and activities the members may also undertake basic maintenance duties, which in a landed club can mean anything from felling trees to fixing a roof to clearing scrub-land.

With such a lot going on accidents can and do happen, and bearing in mind that many nudist camps and sites are situated in secluded or remote areas well away from population centres and proper medical facilities, it's important that they are kept to a minimum. Always follow these guidelines.

- Before joining or visiting any club or nudist resort, check out exactly who is responsible for the insurance, and what is covered, should you have an accident. There may be some sort of national scheme in place as there is in the UK, where BN (British Naturism) insures BN members whilst visiting BN affiliated clubs. The club may have a private insurance scheme, or if not you may be able to arrange your own through a travel agent or specialist broker. Whatever arrangements you make, if you get injured when you're on their premises you want to know who is going to pick up the tab.

- Never do anything that you consider to be dangerous, even if everybody else is doing it. Remember that you may be a long way from any trained medical support.
- Always take proper safety precautions. In particular, wear safety equipment and clothing. This last item does seem to cause some nudists trouble. It sounds like an old joke but we have actually seen a naked man cooking sausages on a barbecue and a naked lady frying eggs on a camping stove. We've also witnessed a naked man chopping logs with an axe and a naked woman clearing thorns and brambles from woodland. She wasn't even wearing gloves for goodness sake! Luckily no one got hurt, but this is just asking for trouble. These people were foolish. Don't be like them.
- Make sure the club or campsite has a properly stocked first aid kit. If not carry an emergency kit yourself, and always take one with you to an unsupervised area such as a nude beach or lakeside.
- Ensure that you, or someone nearby, has a properly working mobile phone. At the very least check whether the club or camp-site has a working payphone. When we first started on the naturist trail very few clubs had payphones (ours still hasn't) and mobiles existed only on *Star Trek* or *The Man From Uncle*. Back then we had no choice. These days, you have no excuse.
- If you suspect that you may be alone at the club or camp-site for a time, and especially if you're intending to stay overnight, take all of the above precautions but also tell someone where you'll be and what time you expect to be back. Many clubs are not visited at all during the week, and if you fall off a roof and break your legs you could be there until the weekend!

We don't want to overplay or exaggerate the danger of accidents. We have never seen anyone have anything other than the smallest of mishaps, but it really is better to be safe than sorry. The list above has been distilled from 30 years accident-free enjoyment of nudist facilities all over the world. Follow it, and keep safe.

Danger from Cold and Hypothermia

Our own feeling is that this section shouldn't really be here. If someone *deliberately* gets naked and cold, and willingly stays naked and cold long enough for it to become a problem, then that person probably hasn't got enough intelligence to undress themselves in the first place. We've never seen it happen, but just in case, let's deal with it.

The rule is simple. Cold is not cool!

We're naturists, not masochists. Rolling naked in the snow is invigorating and running nude in a snowfall is fun, but when you get cold, stop. Go inside and get dressed. Admire the winter wonderland through the clubhouse window with a log fire roaring halfway up the chimney and a glass of something warming in your hand. Chill *out*, don't chill *outside*.

Nudism is no more hazardous to your health than any other outdoor pursuit, and a good deal less dangerous than many. Use your common sense, follow the guidelines above, and stay trouble free as well as clothes-free.

13

Taking The Plunge!

The seven steps to becoming a nudist

So you've read the book, considered the pros and cons, and decided that you'd really like to give naturism a chance. Congratulations, and welcome to the wonderful world of nudism!

But what, exactly, do you do now?

We are about to reveal all. What follows is the definitive, step-by-step, hands-on, hassle-free guide to becoming a nudist.

> The steps outlined here assume that you will be searching, contacting and registering online. If this is not the case, you'll need to substitute the internet references with telephone and snail-mail.

Step One:

Join your national nudist association

You will have gathered by now that we're keen supporters of our national association, and so should you be of yours. Although many nudists now feel that the associations are outdated and increasingly irrelevant, joining should absolutely, positively be your first action as a newcomer. You'll get advice and support, maybe a free magazine as part of your subscription, and you'll also be demonstrating a commitment to the nudist movement.

Even if you anticipate that your nudist career will only ever consist of a few nudist vacations your membership will come in handy. Some clubs and resorts require a valid INF certificate—usually your membership card—before they'll accept a booking, and although your holiday company can usually override this requirement, why take the risk? Besides, your free magazine will contain adverts from the nudist holiday companies and resort reports, so it's definitely worth the subscription fee.

> Some nudist clubs offer a discounted subscription to the relevant national nudist association as part of their membership benefits, so if you're considering joining a club it might be worth checking for any deals first.

Step Two:

Research

Time to use the internet for what it was made for; research, information and communication.

Get online and find out everything you can about naturism and nudism. Try searching your favourite search engine for *nudist clubs* (or *resorts, parks, centres, locations* or *sites* etc.), with perhaps a *UK* or *USA* or similar geographical indicator to narrow the search down to the area you want. Do the same with *nudist beaches, nudist SIGs, nudist organisations,* or whatever it is that you are interested in. Then carry out the same searches using the word *naturist* instead of *nudist*. Being specific in your search terms this way will keep your results more on target than if you were to use a generic keyword such as *nudism* or *naturism*, which will increase your chances of turning up porn or adult sites. We suggest some starter sites in the resources section.

Beware of the nudist forums. Many of them have fallen victim to the porn and get-rich-quick merchants, and those that manage to stay on topic often degenerate into pointless, ill-natured and foul-mouthed slanging matches. They can be useful in small doses but don't take them too seriously—most nudists don't.

Don't rush this step. It's important because it will give you a feel for the nudist movement as a whole and provide more specific information about clubs or beaches and so on that you can use in the next steps.

Step Three:

How involved you want to get?

Now is the time to decide just how committed to the pursuit of naturism you want to become. Your level of dedication will depend entirely on your personal circumstances—how much time you have, how much you're prepared to spend, how far you can travel—and you should consider all of these points carefully before making your decision.

Are you intending to take just the occasional nudist break? Maybe you want to visit a nudist beach once or twice during an otherwise textile vacation? Perhaps you see yourself going nudist more often, regularly using a nudist beach close to home? Or maybe you want to go the whole hog, doing all the above and becoming an active, fee-paying member of a naturist club as well.

Each of these options will make different demands of your time and resources, and if you are to enjoy your naturism to the maximum you need to be realistic in your assessment of what's best for you. Refer back to chapter 4 to remind yourself of some of the pros and cons of restricting your nudism to beaches and vacations or joining a nudist club.

Step four (the final step if you want to be a beach or vacation nudist):

Use the nudist beaches and book your holiday.

That's all there is to it. Using the information gathered from your research, select a suitable beach (is it official, do you require it to have amenities etc.), and just go for it. Remember to obey the etiquette guidelines (see chapter 14), take everything with you that you may need, and just enjoy yourself. Although there's nothing to stop you using each and every nude beach you can find, you might find making friends easier—assuming that's what you want—if you use just one or two beaches on a regular basis.

Step four (if you intend joining a nudist club):

See your national nudist association website or your association magazine

Go through the list of member clubs and visit their websites. See what they have to offer, and get an overall feel for the place. Study them carefully for suitability and then short-list the clubs that most match your requirements. Points you'll need to consider are:

Location

Clubs are often situated in remote areas of the country, with little or no access by public transport, so you will need some way of getting there. Obviously a car is ideal, but at a pinch a cycle will do if the site is within pedalling distance.

Also, bear in mind that the closer a club is to your home, the greater are the chances of meeting someone you know there. This may or may not be a problem for you, but if it is you may want to consider choosing somewhere a little further away. This has actually happened to us several times. Initially it's very embarrassing, especially in the case of professional acquaintances, but you soon realise that you've all been caught quite literally with your pants down and just get on with the fun. The upside is that you grow a local nudist circle, outside the club, made up of friends, neighbours and workmates who all share the same secret.

Facilities

Some clubs own nothing in the way of physical facilities, not even a piece of land. They enjoy their nude time by visiting other clubs and organising swims and saunas. Other clubs have little more than a patch of grass, whilst others are full-blown nude vacation centres.

Deciding what level of amenities you need and are prepared to pay for will help you make your decision.

Whether or not a club has electricity and running water or even a swimming pool might be important to you. Perhaps you need a club that is suitable for the infirm, elderly or disabled, or which offers easy parking. Maybe you want a club-house, or even a bar and catering, or sports facilities, or is pet friendly.

It's worth checking beforehand that the club matches your needs, but be aware that the more you get the more you'll pay!

Cost

Prices can vary widely according to the facilities available. At the time of writing UK club membership fees vary from GBP40 per year (for a small club consisting of a rough lawn in a patch of woodland with no other facilities), to in excess of GBP300 per year (a large resort with all the trimmings). You'll need to weigh the cost against the amount of times you're able or willing to get there. Remember that if you can only use the place four times a year, each visit to a GBP300 club costs you over GBP70, plus your travelling costs. It's a judgement that only you can make, so take your time, and choose wisely.

Sometimes, it's better to choose a less expensive club as your 'main' club, and travel to a larger, better equipped one as a day visitor. This can work out much cheaper over time and may be the best all-round solution for you.

Club Rules

Although these are usually just common sense and rarely burdensome you may need to watch out for them. For instance many clubs prohibit the wearing of piercings, which may be unsuitable for you if you like to sport some prominent steelwork. Some clubs are nude only whilst others are clothing-optional, others still are a mixture of the two. Other things that may influence your choice might be their policy regarding alcohol, smoking and pets, or whether you are required to attend at least one or more work days each year (possibly a problem if you are elderly or infirm).

Club orientation

No, not which way the club faces in relation to the compass. By orientation we mean the attitude to sex and racy behaviour. As we said before, some clubs are very prim and proper whilst others are more liberal. Most are just a happy medium. Make sure you choose the right one. Most importantly make sure you don't join a swingers club by mistake!

Step 5:

Make your selection and email your list

Now you need to actually put pen to paper—or more likely fingers to keypad—and make your interest known. These days nearly all web-sites have a *contact us* button so you can be sure that your message will go to the right person, but please keep the message short and to the point. Most club secretaries are unpaid and hopelessly overworked and won't look favourably on a long and rambling communication.

What should you say? Well, as always, honesty is the best policy. Explain your circumstances, (single man, family group etc.), and that this will be your first experience of naturism. Inform them that you are already a member of your national naturist association—assuming that you are—and quote your membership number. Tell them why you'd like to join their particular club and, especially if you are a single man, indicate any special talents (such as building skills—see chapter 8) that you can offer. Finish with your full name and your return e-mail address. Last of all, re-read the message, make sure it's accurate, run a spell-check over it and press *send*. Job done!

Here are some additional points to bear in mind.

If you are a single man and your single status is, shall we say, less than straightforward, be honest and say so. For instance, if you are actually a married man but your wife is not interested in joining, tell them. Remember what we said about this in chapter 8? It might seem easier to say nothing, but it never, ever, works out in the end.

If you don't receive an immediate reply, don't assume the worst. Remember those poor overburdened club secretaries? Allow up to two weeks for an acknowledgement, then send a gentle reminder. Above all, don't pester and don't get abusive.

You needn't restrict yourself to applying to just one club, or even one club at a time. If several meet your criteria, apply to them all. The more you're in the more you win as they say, and if you keep on trying you will be successful eventually.

Step Six:

Just wait and see what happens next

Crunch time! There really is little more you can do at this stage, except sit back and wait to find out whether or not your efforts have been rewarded.

You shouldn't have to wait too long. Although the actual procedures vary from club to club and from country to country, ultimately you will receive one of three answers, which will tell you that:

1) Your application has been denied, or

2) You have been placed on the dreaded waiting list and will be contacted again if and when a place becomes available, or

3) You have been invited to move along to the next stage of the membership process. It's unlikely that you'll be granted membership on the basis of your initial enquiry email alone— there's always at least one more stage.

If either 1) or 2) happens, I'm afraid there's not much else you can do, except be thankful for the fact that you've applied to more than one club. (You have, haven't you?)

Step Seven:

Join and enjoy

Once your membership application has been accepted in principle the next stage will consist of one, all, or a combination of the following.

- You will be invited to visit the site.
- A club official will visit you at home.
- You will be invited to join, asked to complete a membership form and pay the subscription.
- Your first visit as a member

Not every club will do all of these things, but most will do at least two of them. (And every club will ask you to pay the membership fee.)

Let's look at them all.

You will be invited to visit the site

Nowadays it's more common to be asked to visit the site than to be visited by a club official at home. If you have applied as a married couple you will both need to attend, and your membership application may be refused if you don't; quite naturally the club needs to be sure that you both know about, and are happy to continue with, the membership process.

This is a chance for you to inspect what the club has to offer, to meet the officials and maybe some of the members, and for the committee to meet you. Take the opportunity to have a good look round, and don't be frightened to ask questions. It may be wise to think about and write out a list of questions and concerns before you go, so that you don't experience the *I wish I'd asked that* feeling experienced by less organised folks. Remember what we said about making sure the club suits your needs? Well, now is the time to find out. Check out how closely the amenities match your wish list. For instance:

- Has it got running water, and how will you cope if it hasn't?
- What are the toilets like—and has it even got toilets?
- Are the members on average younger or older, and how does this match your own profile and comfort level?
- What about child or sports facilities?
- What are your duties as a member? Remember that if it's a members' club there may be a requirement to help out with the chores. Have you the time or the physical ability to do this?
- What is the policy on smoking, drinking or pets, if this is an issue with you?
- Are the grounds adequately screened?

And so on.

Remember that you will be paying good money—sometimes lots of it—for the privilege of becoming a member, and you don't want to waste your hard earned cash. To make the best possible start you'll want to make sure you know what you're getting for your money, and that what you're getting is what you want, before you commit yourself.

A club official will visit you at home

If you are asked to accept a home visit from a club official, don't worry. This isn't an excuse to poke about your home or to discover what sort of neighbourhood you live in. It's simply an opportunity for the membership committee to check that the details you gave about yourself are correct. It will provide confirmation that you are who you say you are and that you've given the correct address.

Once again, if you have applied as a married couple you will both need to be there. During this visit you will probably be asked a few questions and get a chance to ask a few of your own. You will usually be shown a few photographs—or more likely these days a DVD or Powerpoint presentation—and if everything goes well you'll be invited to visit the club.

Don't feel angry or insulted about this home visit; if it's club policy it will apply to all new applicants, and is no reflection on you. We were visited at home when we first applied to join a club, and Liz had palpitations for days beforehand worrying that the people would turn up stark naked, or with nudist stickers all over the car, or otherwise alarm the neighbours. We needn't have been concerned. The whole thing was as innocuous as a Baptist meeting but considerably quieter and much shorter!

Nowadays, as we've mentioned, the home visit is a rarity, which is a great pity. It's an unfortunate fact that the nudist movement does attract some undesirable people, and the home visit definitely helped to weed out these before they caused a problem.

You will be invited to join, asked to complete a membership form and pay the subscription

Many clubs operate some sort of probationary system, under which new members can have their membership revoked should they misbehave during the trial period.

The last stage in your enrolment is the easiest. You'll be informed by letter or email that your application has been accepted. It only remains for you to pay the membership fee and you're ready for:

Your first visit as a member

If you've already experienced social nudity on a nude beach or on vacation, your first visit to the club may not be too daunting. If this is going to be your first ever taste of public nudity, however, the realisation will probably cause you some serious trepidation, and you will no doubt find many urgent and compelling reasons to delay or postpone your visit. This is a perfectly natural reaction, but please, fight against it. You've come a long way to get here. Don't let it be a wasted effort. If you fail now you probably won't ever find the necessary strength or courage to carry this through. We've all managed it. You can too!

Here are some final guidelines.

- If the club is not permanently manned, and you don't yet have a key, phone ahead to make sure someone will be there to let you in. Sounds obvious but we know one couple (ahem!) who once endured a six hour return car journey for the pleasure of waiting outside a locked gate in the middle of nowhere.

- Take with you everything you're going to need. If it's your first time naked take a 'security' blanket to pull over you the first couple of times you meet someone.
- Leave the camera behind!
- Don't be pushy, but don't be unfriendly either. Sounds hard, but it's no different to meeting new friends in any other social situation, and you've done that before haven't you?
- Observe the nudist etiquette, and obey club rules.
- Take your litter home with you.

And that, friends, is how to become a nudist. Welcome. You now belong to a very distinguished minority!

14

Etiquette Matters. . .

. . .even when you're naked!

In common with other special interest groups, nudists have developed a set of unofficial rules which define what constitutes good manners and acceptable behaviour within the nudist context. These are by no means burdensome or difficult to remember, and if you act with the same courtesy and respect towards others that you would while clothed you shouldn't have a problem. However, they are designed to make life more pleasant for all of us, and by adhering to these guidelines you will enhance your own nudist pleasure. Here are some to remember.

Always use your own towel when sitting on a seat or other hard surface

This is simply good hygiene, and shows a proper respect for the property of others. A towel isn't strictly necessary if you are sat directly on the grass or sand, but this is not something we recommend anyway.

Do not take nude photographs of anybody—especially children —without permission

> We would advise against taking nude photos of children at *any* time.

Many nudists are terrified of their pictures being published anywhere, but especially on the internet. For this reason the majority of private clubs forbid photography altogether, and although it's not possible to ban photography on a public beach you must respect the concerns of others and their right to privacy. Which brings us neatly to the next point.

Respect the privacy of others

Don't sit too close to others, especially if you don't know them, and don't stare unduly. Be friendly, but not forward and don't intrude on conversations. If and when you strike up a conversation with other naturists don't ask personal questions or ask for personal details. Most nudists will happily tell you their first names but are uneasy about divulging their surname, hometown or occupation etc. to strangers, and resent being asked to do so.

Once you have made nudist friends, never divulge the fact that they are nudists to anyone else. *You* might be happy to proclaim your nudism to anyone who will listen, but other nudists may be more reticent. If they want anyone else to know, they'll tell them themselves.

Bring your own supplies

Especially towel, sunscreen, beach umbrella, food, drinks, tissues, first-aid kit, money. Remember that many clubs are buried deep in the back-country and most nudist beaches have little in the way of amenities, so be prepared. If you do get caught short you will invariably find someone to help you, but it's better not to impose on the hospitality of others. (See Appendix 2)

Do not behave in a lewd or offensive manner

The cause of genuine naturism has suffered significantly recently from the spread of the public-sex-and-flash-mob, who are steadily crawling out of their dingy cellars and onto our sunny nudist places. Their debased activities have triggered so many complaints from the public that some of our most treasured and well-established naturist beaches have now been closed for naturist use, and others are under threat. They are few in number compared to the many thousands of genuine naturists, but the damage they do is great and all real nudists suffer, not only in terms of lost beaches but by association in the public mind with such creatures.

Needless to say these people are not naturists, just deviants using our name and places and they are not welcome at any time. But sadly sometimes it's not just the out and out swingers who transgress.

Unfortunately some misguided individuals believe that the relaxed dress code of a nudist club or beach gives them a licence to indulge in behaviour which would be unacceptable anywhere else. It does not, it is not tolerated and it could get you banned or even locked up!

Examples of this sort of behaviour include:

- Indulging in sexual activity.
- Deliberately positioning yourself in a provocative or obscene pose.
- Encouraging or flaunting an erection. (See chapter 8.)
- Urinating in full view of others. (Yes, unfortunately we've seen that done, by both sexes!)
- Being uncouth or loutish.

Just don't do it!

(Incidentally, here's a nice point of nudist etiquette to for you to ponder. Could massaging sun-cream into your female partner's breasts or bottom be interpreted as indulging in sexual activity? It's a common enough sight on a nudist beach, and it's something we do ourselves, but is it a breach of etiquette? We think it's a matter of degree. A certain amount of mild contact is necessary, but a full-on groping session would probably be considered inappropriate!)

Don't gawk

It is impolite, and could result in you going home with a black eye. If you just want to ogle naked people stay at home and dribble over some internet sleaze.

Do not excessively encourage others to get naked – your motives may be misunderstood

People may think that you are just a little too interested in seeing them naked. Conversely, do not attend a nudist beach or club and stay clothed yourself whilst others get naked, unless you have a very good reason. It would certainly be considered impolite and would probably arouse suspicion.

Be aware of any beach or club rules, and obey them

For instance some beaches ban pets, alcohol, music, or the lighting of fires. Some clubs operate a total nudity policy, others are more clothes-optional. However much you may agree or disagree with the rules, they are there for a reason. If you don't like them, don't turn up.

Get dressed before you leave

Otherwise you stand the risk of getting arrested, and of bringing naturism into disrepute.

On a secluded beach which is not specifically naturist, leave a bathing suit on a rock to let others know they are approaching an unclothed person. If you don't and you're sunbathing in a quiet location, others might come upon you suddenly and accidentally. If you're uncomfortable having your suit out of reach, bring a spare.

On an exposed beach, position yourself in the open so you can see people coming

Because you'll have chance to put something on before they get there if you need to.

And last but not least...

Be a responsible nudist and citizen

Illegal or irresponsible activity can get clothing-optional beaches and clubs closed. Take your litter home with you. Park in the designated areas only. Obey any rules, bye-laws or restrictions. Remind others of proper etiquette if necessary and appropriate, and report any illegal or irresponsible activity to the proper authorities. Remember that in many locations the right to go nude has been hard won, and is constantly under threat. Do your part to secure the future of naturism.

15

Frequently Asked Questions

Bare Faqs

Here are some of the questions we've been most frequently asked over the years. Some of them have already been covered in this book, others appear here for the first time. If you have any questions which you think should be included in future editions of this book, please email us using the contact form on our blog at (*http://lovenaturism.com/?p=50*).

Do I have to get naked?

Well that is the general idea isn't it? If you're not joining to get naked, why are you joining? Perhaps you should question your reasons for wanting to join.

Sorry. What I meant was 'do I have to get naked all the time?'

In a nudist situation you should strip off whenever you can, but we're naturists not fanatics and there will be times when it's not convenient or appropriate to do so, for instance when it's too cold.

Where it is acceptable but not compulsory to go naked, as in a clothes-optional environment, you should strip off whenever possible, as not doing so could:

- Increase the ratio of clothed people to nude people to an extent that causes the nudists to stay away, which in turn could result in the loss of the clothes-optional ambience of the location or event.
- Cause others to view your presence there with suspicion.

Some private clubs are *full-nude*, where nudity is mandatory at all times, whilst others—perhaps the majority—operate a sort of hybrid system that allows some leeway in respect of clothing but insist on full nudity at the pool and full dress in the restaurant. It sounds a little crazy, but it does make some sense and generally it works quite well.

Usually you should follow the custom of wherever it is you are visiting. As in most things in life you'll find it easier if you go with the flow.

How worried should I be about getting an erection?

This has been covered more comprehensively in another section, but in brief don't worry. Erections are rare, but if you do experience one:

- Take a dip in the cold pool (or ocean or whatever) If this is not possible, take your mind off it by thinking of poverty, war, politicians or something equally as unpleasant.
- Satisfy yourself that your fellow naturists are themselves acting in a genuine naturist manner. If they are not—leave.
- If the symptoms persist examine your real reasons for becoming a naturist. Don't confuse naturism with exhibitionism and voyeurism or sex and pornography. If this is really what you want, admit it to yourself and join something more appropriate.

On my first visit will I have to go nude right away?

Probably not, but you can always check ahead to ask what their policy is. As far as I know even clubs that rigidly enforce the nudity rule will give you some time to get used to your new surroundings and ambience.

Are pets allowed?

At some places yes, at others no. It depends upon the club rules or local bye-laws, so check before you go. In any event you should keep your pet on a lead at all times and clear up any mess it may make.

What about alcohol, smoking, or music?

Again this will vary from place to place. There is unlikely to be any restriction on these at a public nude beach as long as you don't annoy others (for instance the playing of loud music is usually prohibited and if you stagger around drunk you'll be asking for trouble). Most private clubs take a similarly relaxed view—in fact sharing a glass or two of wine with friends is part of the nudist culture—but a minority of clubs will not countenance some or all of these activities on site, so make sure that you are aware of the club policy before you join.

I have a genital piercing. Will this be a problem?

Probably not on a public nude beach, but many private clubs prohibit them. Once again, check in advance.

What if I'm shaved, or tattooed?

Being a *smoothie* or tattooed is not usually a problem, unless the tattoo is offensive or obscene, in which case you might be asked to cover up.

Do I have to get undressed in full view of everybody?

Most nudists do, but you don't have to. This is a common question, especially from ladies, who may be happy to consider getting naked in company but tremble at the thought of actually stripping in public! It's a concern that disappears with experience but if it's an anxiety of yours don't worry. If you're at a club or beach you can change into a tracksuit or beach-dress in your car and slip it off when you're ready, and most sauna-swim locations provide changing cubicles. Either way, it's unlikely that anyone else will even notice.

I have children by a former marriage. Can I bring them?

Children are usually welcome, but for legal reasons clubs are increasingly insisting on written consent from the other parent before they'll allow the children to attend.

I am married, but my wife isn't interested in nudism. Can I join a club as a single man?

We would strongly advise against this. We discuss this more fully in chapter 8.

Am I allowed to try and date someone I meet in a nudist environment?

Of course! Many nudist relationships start this way. Just obey the normal dictates of good manners, respect and consideration. 'Coming on strong' is no more acceptable—and just as likely to fail—in a nudist situation as in any other.

What will people say when they find out I'm a naturist?

They won't know unless you decide to tell them.

Is nudism a religion?

No. It is a leisure activity, or to some a way of life, just like golf, or fishing, and as such is compatible with the teachings of most of the world's major religions.

Would I be allowed to take photographs in a nudist situation?

This is a difficult one to answer as it depends on many things. Lots of nudists dread their photograph appearing in public, especially on the internet, and as a result many nudist areas and events ban photography within their own areas. Others allow the taking of photos in designated spots only. As a general rule, don't take photps of anyone unless you have their express permission, and then only if there is no other nudist about—otherwise you and your camera might take an unplanned swim. Don't take nude pictures of children, full stop.

If nudism is so great, why can't I just do it at home, on my own?

You can. Most nudists do, sometimes. However remember that not everyone is able to. Perhaps they share a house with others, or maybe they have no garden, or there's some other reason why they need to travel somewhere where they can practice naturism safely.

Also, don't forget that we are social creatures and like to mix with others of our own kind. We can eat at home, but most of choose to dine out from time to time. We can watch the match on television, but we still go to the stadium. And even if we're able to go nudist at home, it's nice to go to the beach or the club sometimes.

16

Nudists in their own words.

Your chance to meet real life nudists

What follows are just some of the responses to a survey that we set up specifically to obtain information for this book. We've only room to include a small sampling of the complete survey and for the sake of brevity we've had to trim some of the replies.

These are real nudists, and these are their own words, just as they wrote them, although some have used fake names. We hope that you'll find their comments interesting, illuminating and useful.

Sepp and Mary
Age: 42 and 40.
Situation: M/F married couple
Nudist for: 5 years

Tell us how you became involved in naturism

We wandered onto a nudist beach by accident on vacation in the Canary Islands. There was no marker. One minute we were on an ordinary beach and the next everyone was naked! Mary is American and was quite shocked, but I am German and didn't find it at all unusual. Mary wanted to turn around and go back, but I persuaded her to stay whilst I did some nude sunbathing. We kept as far as we could from the others, and Mary kept her swimsuit on all afternoon. Later that evening we got friendly with another couple, who told us that they often used another nude beach a little way along the coast. We went with them a couple of times, and gradually Mary lost her swimsuit. Now we are both hooked!

What is the best thing about naturism?

The people. Mostly they are so nice.

What is the worst thing about naturism?

Usually the men outnumber the women, and sometimes some of them seem to be there for the wrong reason.

What advice would you give to someone wishing to become a nudist?

If you're wondering about it, just do it. It won't hurt you, and if you don't like it you can just stop.

DaNude1

Age: 38
Status: M/F married couple
Nudist for: 22 years

Tell us how you became involved in naturism

Accidentally ordered a Lee Baxandall's *World Guide to Nude Beaches and Resorts* when I was a teenager and read about the philosophy of naturism and have been a faithful happy participant ever since.

What is the best thing about naturism?

No false fronts, no classes of people, other people accept you at face value.

What is the worst thing about naturism?

That it is not more prevalent and well accepted and mainstream.

What advice would you give to someone wishing to become a nudist?

Just be yourself— if you try to put on 'airs' it will eventually catch up with you.

Clay and Stephen

Age: 36 and 35
Status: M/M relationship
Nudist for: 2 years

Tell us how you became involved in naturism

It was a deliberate, carefully considered decision on our part. We've both always been very conscious of our health, and we try to maintain optimum health in the most natural way. We decided to include naturism in our natural health lifestyle after reading about the healing power of sunlight and vitamin D on a natural health website.

After some research, (including reading your book), we decided to embrace naturism for health, and we're so glad we did.

What is the best thing about naturism?

The feeling of liberation and well-being which it creates.

What is the worst thing about naturism?

The behaviour of a minority of other so-called naturists who use being nude as an excuse for public sexual displays which reflect badly on naturism and causes all naturists to be tarnished as perverts and weirdos.

What advice would you give to someone wishing to become a nudist?

Be open and upfront. As a gay couple we were worried that we would never be accepted into 'mainstream' naturism, so we joined a gay nudist organisation initially. Although the guys were pleasant we felt that the emphasis was more on being gay than nudity for health. We realise that this is probably not everybody's experience, but it was the way we felt. We then applied to join a mixed-gender club here on the west coast, and as we were completely honest about our relationship we didn't expect to be accepted. To our amazement we were accepted straight off, and since then no one, including us, has mentioned our sexual orientation. We are just accepted for who we are.

Geoff from Newcastle (Australia)

Age: 48
Status: M/F married couple
Nudist for: 33 years

Tell us how you became involved in naturism

In my first year in high school, a member of my class skinny-dipped on a school beach excursion. I remember thinking, 'That must be fun!' but I didn't try it then. I did, however, start going nude at home whenever I was alone. I didn't know what my parents would think if they found out.

When I went to university, I discovered that quite a few people were quite open about nudity. One of the girls in my year had actually done some nude modelling, and had gone to campus functions wearing very little and conveniently losing her costume during the evening. I found out that she actually went to a nude beach in the area with her boyfriend and some other people they knew, so I started going nude at the beach too. It was the most natural thing to do.

I was also one of only a few males at the beach who usually shaved their pubic hair. It was the mid 1970s, so I guess I was an early 'smoothie', though I didn't remove all of my body hair. I also had a girlfriend then who wasn't afraid to go nude outdoors and who also shaved her pubic hair. I've continued to be a 'partial smoothie' (shaving pubic hair only) and these days I'm nude at home when I can.

What is the best thing about naturism?

It's the feeling of being able to be completely open with others. You're not able to hide behind anything. Naturism is all about accepting yourself as you are, and by doing that, realising you should also do the same for others.

What is the worst thing about naturism?

Some people associate naturism with kinky sex, and see it as a perversion. Sure, being nude is sensual, and also sexual sometimes, but sex is as much a part of life as eating or sleeping.

This can mean that sometimes it makes for difficult situations in relationships with other people. Not everyone understands if you tell them you're a naturist.

What advice would you give to someone wishing to become a nudist?

Go nude at home first, before trying anything public. Start off by sleeping nude, and spending time nude before going to work, and after coming home.

If you have a partner, let them know you like being nude. Don't hide it!

If your partner won't try going nude, don't pressure him-her. Just continue to go nude yourself as often as you can without causing any offence.

Once you're confident about being nude in public, give it a try at a nude beach or club/resort. This is all the better if your partner will join you. Many clubs or resorts won't admit males who don't have partners staying with them.

How has naturism affected your relationship?

My wife initially thought that wanting to go nude was some sort of sexual perversion. Fortunately, she has learned that being nude together is great for relationships. She still hasn't been able to cast aside her poor body image, though, so any public nudity for her is out of the question. She has skinny-dipped with me in a country stream though, which was a wonderful experience! She even got undressed more quickly than I did!

These days, I can stand around nude and talk to her, and she doesn't insist that I get dressed. I don't go nude all the time, though.

Anything else?

Remember that when you spend time nude you are more at one with the world. You'll feel the breeze, the sun, the rain, the ocean in a way that you can't experience clothed. Just do it!

If you're male, don't worry about erections. Sure, they'll happen sometimes, but they aren't a major issue!

When you spend time nude with members of the opposite sex in non-sexual situations, you won't be aroused in the way you might be in the bedroom with your partner. No doubt it will be a pleasant experience, but you won't be viewing them as sex objects. Naturism creates a healthy respect for others, body, soul and mind!

Larry

Age: 53
Status: M/F married couple
Nudist for: 30+ years

Tell us how you became involved in naturism

For most of my adult life I served in the USAF all over the world. While serving in Germany I was introduced to nudism-naturism by my girlfriend and her family. It opened my mind and my spirit and from that time I have been a practicing nudist/naturist for 30+ yrs. When I get out of my clothes it is like taking the weight of the world off my shoulders.

What is the best thing about naturism?

Meeting people who are proud of who they are and what they believe in. This has enriched my life. When you can look a person (male or female) in the eye and be comfortable with your self and others around you. That is the best thing about naturism.

What is the worst thing about naturism?

Changes in climate while traveling.

What advice would you give to someone wishing to become a nudist?

Talk to people who are nudist for their point of view. Go to a beach or resort to see if being nude is right for you.

Gina from Ostend.
Age: 36.
Status: Single (divorced) female
Nudist for: 7 years

Tell us how you became involved in naturism

After my divorce some years ago I went on vacation with a girlfriend to Majorca. I'd not done nudity before in public, but now in trying out new experiences we tried the nude beach at Es Trenc. I loved the free feeling of me, and when returned home I went nudist as often as possible.

There is now a nude beach near my home at Bredene near Ostend which make me happy because it is so close and I can use it when the weather is good.

What is the best thing about naturism?

The free feeling of the weather on my body, the freshness of a nudist day.

What is the worst thing about naturism?

That sometimes people think you are a little crazy in going nude.

What advice would you give to someone wishing to become a nudist?

Don't wait, do it at this moment.

How has naturism affected your relationship?

I remain in a divorce, but have many nice nudist friends and maybe will one day marry a nice nudist man. Thank you for nudisme for making me happy again!

Susan (Australia)

Age:24
Status: Single female
Nudist for: 2 years

Tell us how you became involved in naturism

I've always had a strong desire to get back to nature, and although my lifestyle doesn't give me too much opportunity I try to connect with the natural world as often as I can. The idea of naturism has actually appealed to me for a long time, but it was only quite recently that I decided to try it.

My first choice was to try a nudist beach, but I found out about a nudist swim that was taking place in my area, so I went along there. Although it felt a bit weird at first, (geeeze, we all had to undress in the same locker room and I was surrounded by strange men seeing my underwear and then some!) it was quite fun and very empowering.

Now I mostly use the nude beach, where I regularly go with some friends, but we still occasionally use the swim and have week-ended at some clubs.

What is the best thing about naturism?

From my point of view it was a body image thing. I thought that I was a little overweight, but I'd never really had a chance to compare against other women, in the nude anyway. Now I realise that my body is normal and really quite good and I have in fact lost 12 pounds in weight. I really feel good about myself.

It also feels soooo good to feel the elements against your skin. I guess the word is empowering.

What is the worst thing about naturism?

The ratio of men to women. I knew that there would be more men than women, but it seems as if it's about 10 to 1 sometimes. If I hadn't been so keen to try nudism I don't think I would have come back after the first day at the swim. Come on girls, we need you!

What advice would you give to someone wishing to become a nudist?

Don't be put off by what I've written. Try it ladies. You will love it!

Anything else?

Try getting nude in Australia. It's perfect.

David
Age 66
Status M/F married couple
Nudist for: 50 years

Tell us how you became involved in naturism

I was a naturist before I knew the word, from the age of about 10. We lived very near a 10 sq.m. natural park, and I used to wander in it, skinny-dip in the pools, commune with the wildlife. I have been a practising naturist ever since.

What is the best thing about naturism?

Not having a wet swimsuit.

What is the worst thing about naturism?

The closed minds of some bureaucratic club officials.

What advice would you give to someone wishing to become a nudist?

Go to a deserted spot and take your clothes off; let the sun shine on your naked body. Then try it at a nude beach or naturist sauna, and you'll realise that other people are a comfort, not a threat. Then you're a naturist. Go for it!

How has naturism affected your relationship?

My wife is totally comfortable with pubic nudity, so long as there are other naturists around. In fact, she does not possess a swimsuit, so will only go to a beach if it is a naturist one. There are no problems, only benefits. We go naked at home.

Nude Bob
Age: 37
Status: M/F married couple
Nudist for: 20 years

Tell us how you became involved in naturism

It just seemed like a completely natural thing to do – it was so relaxing to take off my clothes

What is the best thing about naturism?

Everyone is treated as a human being and having no clothes on seems to allow adults to act like kids (ie. have fun and not care what anyone else is thinking.)

What is the worst thing about naturism?

That it is not completely accepted as normal and healthy, and the stigma that unenlightened people attach to it.

What advice would you give to someone wishing to become a nudist?

Go for it – you'll look back and wonder why you waited so long.

How has naturism affected your relationship?

My eternal wish is that my wife would *embrace* nudism rather than reluctantly joining in every now and then.

Anything else?

Nudism would go a long way to solving a lot of the problems we have in the world at the moment, not only in terms of tolerance of others but also acceptance of yourself.

Peter from the US

Age:54
Status: Single male
Nudist for: 14 years

Tell us how you became involved in naturism

I'd always liked to go nude, ever since I was a small boy and my mom would tell me off for taking off my PJ's during the night. As I got older and moved away from home, I used to go about nude in my apartment, but I never went nude in a social situation. Then one day I was working on a navy contract in San Diego and one of the guys I was working with told me that he liked to go hang gliding of the cliffs overlooking the ocean. What intrigued me most though was that he said that nudists used the beach below the hang gliding point. I went with him one afternoon, pretending to be interested in the hang gliding, but actually to scout out the location of the beach. A couple of days later I went to the beach on my own. It is called Blacks Beach. It was pretty strange at first to get undressed, but what was the most embarrassing wasn't getting nude in front of the nudists but in front of the surfers, who also used the beach and mingled with the nudists!

Anyway, I've been a regular nudist ever since. I just wished I tried it sooner.

What is the best thing about naturism?

The feeling of freedom and liberty that comes with taking off your clothes.

What is the worst thing about naturism?

Being a single man a lot of people think that you're just after a cheap look at nude women! Also it's difficult to get accepted into some clubs.

What advice would you give to someone wishing to become a nudist?

Don't wait until it's too late. Just go and do it.

Dave

Age: 57
Status: Single male
Nudist for: 30+ years

Tell us how you became involved in naturism

With great difficulty! I first tried back in the early 70s. At that time in the UK nude beaches were rare, nudist holidays were rare *and* expensive and the only feasible way to go nudist was to join a club.

After some difficulty I found out about CCBN, the UK nudist Federation, and I wrote to them asking for details. I then applied to three different clubs. Two told me that there were no vacancies for single men and I didn't hear from the third at all.

However, CCBN had sent me a copy of their magazine and I saw an advert for a club called Eureka, which appeared to have few membership restrictions, so I applied and was duly accepted as a twenty something single man. What a great thrill! My first visit there was an amazing experience, the people were friendly and fun and I used the club on a regular basis for some years. Some of my fondest nudist memories lie there.

Sadly the club folded on the death of its owner, and although by this time nude beaches and holidays were more commonplace I missed the companionship of club life, and started re-applying again. Guess what? More stonewalling, only this time I was told that I'd be placed on a waiting list.

To cut a long story short I eventually have become a member of a club again, but only through a contact I met at Studland Beach. (*A UK nudist beach.*) I am very happy there, but oh how I miss Eureka!

What is the best thing about naturism?

The people you meet.

What is the worst thing about naturism?

The attitude of some nudists towards single men. The attitude of the media and the outside world towards naturists.

What advice would you give to someone wishing to become a nudist?

Don't be put off by anything. If you want to do it, keep trying. Make plenty of contacts.

Anything else?

Support your nudist Federation. They could be a great help to you, and these days with the internet it's so easy.

17

Endpiece

'What spirit is so empty and blind, that it cannot recognize the fact that the foot is more noble than the shoe, and skin more beautiful that the garment with which it is clothed?'

Michelangelo

'Your clothes conceal much of your beauty, yet they hide not the unbeautiful. And though you seek in garments the freedom of privacy, you may find in them a harness and a drain. Would that you could meet the sun and the wind with more of your body and less of your raiment.'

Khalil Gibran, *The Prophet*

'But for me, being naked out of doors and in the water is one of the best ways I have ever found to restore my sense of blissful innocence. It takes me back to that place of my almost forgotten childhood, where I got to run around undressed without anyone telling me I had to cover up or be embarrassed.'

Elizabeth Rosner, *Notes on Nude-Beach Season*, *'Los Angeles Times'*, *August 12, 2006.*

Thanks for staying until the end. I hope your journey has been interesting, enjoyable and a lot of fun.

Hopefully this book has given you the inspiration and information to start your new life as a nudist. You are about to embark on a fascinating journey, during which you will meet many new friends and travel to many fabulous locations. It may seem a strange place at first, but this book has given you all the knowledge you need to walk in this fantastic new world with confidence, poise and ease. We have given you the inside information. The rest is up to you.

Bon Voyage, and if you meet us on your journey, be sure to say hello!

Liz and James Egger,

October 2015.

Glossary

What do they mean by that?

Like most other special interest groups, the nudist movement uses terms that may bewilder the newcomer. Here are some of the most common.

AANR

The initials of the *American Association for Nude Recreation,* one of the largest of the associations representing US nudists. AANR is divided into seven regions and currently charters around 259 nudist resorts and campgrounds across the United States. In September 2010 it withdrew its association with the International Naturist Federation, accusing the INF of being 'eurocentric'.

BN

Initials of *British Naturism* (formerly the *Central Council for British Naturism* or *CCBN*), which is the national nudist association for the UK and also the title of its quarterly magazine.

Body Painting

A form of body art where designs are painted directly onto the skin. Inevitably, body painting artists and exhibitions proliferate at commercial nudist resorts, where the prospect of unlimited willing human canvasses offers a tempting source of income to struggling body painters, who, incidentally, are rarely nudists themselves.

Whilst some of the effects are undoubtedly striking and colourful, body painting as a nudist activity is frowned upon in the more traditional naturist circles as it is impossible to paint someone without touching them, and touching a stranger, especially on the erogenous zones (to which, it has to be said, many of the designs draw attention), is considered to be unacceptable.

Clothes Optional or CO

A location or an event at which nudity is accepted, or even encouraged, but is not mandatory. A common example of a clothing-optional area would be a nude beach, whilst The Burning Man Festival, held every year in the Nevada desert is a good example of a clothes-optional event.

(*Find out more about the annual* Burning Man Festival at *http://en.wikipedia.org/wiki/Burning_man*)

Colony

As in *nudist colony*. Although popular with non-nudists, this term is rarely, if ever used by nudists, who prefer the expressions *nudist site, nudist club*, or *nudist resort*. Oddly, even non-naturists rarely refer to a *naturist* colony.

FKK

Short for *Freikörperkultur* (Free Body Culture), the German nudist movement. Frequently seen on signs at European beaches indicating that it is nude or clothes-optional.

Gawker

In a nudist context this is a creature who stares and spies on naked bodies, usually on a beach and often from hiding, for its own sexual gratification. It used to be called a *Peeping Tom*. The *Merriam-Webster* online dictionary defines a gawker as someone who stares at someone in a rude and stupid way, which, as anyone who has ever witnessed a line of these drooling oafs will know, is a perfect description.

Gay Nudists

The gay nudist faction has, in recent years, emerged as an important and growing sub-community within the wider nudist movement, possibly as a result of the difficulties faced by single men attempting to join the mainstream nudist community. Many traditional nudists have mixed feelings about such groups, taking the view that a nudist group based upon sexual orientation runs counter to the underlying philosophy of nudism.

INF

The initials of the *International Naturist Federation* (also known by its French name of *Federation Naturiste Internationale*, or FNI). The INF is the international umbrella naturist organisation, based in Antwerp, which co-ordinates and facilitates communication between the national nudist federations and associations. (Although not the *AANR*. See above.)

Landed

As in *landed club*. A club that has its own piece of real estate, whether owned or rented, at which its members can enjoy getting naked. Landed clubs can be as small as a private lawn or as big as a large estate and every size in between.

The opposite of a landed club is, of course, a *non-landed club*, which doesn't have any grounds of its own but whose members regularly meet at different locations specially hired for the occasion, or enjoy group visits to landed clubs. Most *swim/sauna* groups fall into this category.

Miniten

A game popular with nudists, similar to tennis but played with solid faced bats on a smaller court.

Nakation

A nakation is a relatively new word simply meaning a *clothing optional vacation*. Even though nudists have been going on nude cruises and vacations for many years, the word *nakation* seems to have sparked media and social interest in a way that the term *nude vacation* never did.

Nudist or naturist (also nudism or naturism)

A person who goes nude in social and usually mixed gender groups, specifically in cultures where this is not the norm. Some traditionalists insist that there is a subtle difference between the two terms, a nudist being someone who practices simple nudity whilst a naturist practises social nudity within a wider philosophy that may also embrace environmentalism or vegetarianism. It's an interesting point of view, but we think it's a bit precious. There is a tendency to use the word *nudist* in the USA and *naturist* in the rest of the world, but otherwise the terms are identical and can be interchanged freely.

Petanque

Another very popular naturist game. Petanque is a form of boules where the goal is to throw metal balls as close as possible to a jack, which is a small wooden target ball. (*More about* petanque *at http://en.wikipedia.org/wiki/Petanque)*

Piercings

In a nudist context this usually means nipple or genital piercings. It's probably worth repeating that piercings are not universally appreciated in the nudist world. Nothing gets naturists of a certain disposition so bent out of shape as an erogenous zone punctured by a little bit of metal.

Whilst a set of tinware would probably raise few eyebrows and fewer objections on an unregulated nudist beach, it might cause the membership committee of some clubs to blow a fuse, so for the sake of their blood-pressure as well as your own harmonious integration into the group check the club's policy before you join.

Sauna/swim

A nudist get-together at a suitable municipal or private premises for an evening's nude recreation. These often take place at local authority swimming baths which have been hired for the purpose. Attendance is usually by invitation only, and a small cover charge is required to defray costs.

Skinny-Dipping

Swimming or bathing naked.

Smoothie

Someone who shaves off much of his or her body hair, especially from around the pubic region.

Textile

A non-nudist. (As in *He's a textile*, or *This is a textile beach*.)

Topless or top-free

A location at which women are 'allowed' to bare their breasts (for instance a topless beach), or the act of doing so (as in *I went topless on holiday*).

Toplessness is allowed at many locations where full nudity is prohibited and is almost universally practised on European beaches. *Top-free* is the preferred term in North America.

Appendix 2

What to take with you

There's more to travelling light than you think!

Many nudist sites and beaches are in remote areas and may not offer much in the way of facilities, so you should take with you everything you may need. Naturally this will depend upon what's available at your destination, but the following list will give you a guide as to what you should take as a minimum.

A satnav / good map / guidebook / directions

Nudist locations are often situated in hard-to-find places. Also a nudist beach might occupy only a designated section of a much larger textile beach. You'll avoid hours of frustration (and possibly tons of embarrassment) if you know where you're going, and you go to the right spot when you get there!

Sufficient food and drink for your stay

Assuming you are unable or do not want to obtain refreshment on site.

A beach umbrella and / or windbreak if applicable, plus any leisure furniture

A beach umbrella is very important if you are going to spend any length of time on an exposed and sunny beach, especially if you've got children with you.

Avoid the cheap supermarket makes; they're usually too small, too flimsy and only offer a little shade, not real UV protection. Spend a little more and buy something like the Coolibar Titanium, (*www.coolibar.com*) which has a UV protection factor of 50+ and is sturdy enough to cope with most normal beach conditions.

Towel(s)

At least one for sitting on, maybe another one if you are intending to swim.

Tracksuit or similar, and sandals or flip-flops

Ideal if you want to cover up quickly without the bother of getting fully dressed.

Hat, sunglasses, sun-cream and lip-block

Be safe in the sun.

Money

Just in case. Take enough for your needs, but not so much that it becomes a security problem.

Mobile phone

Vital in case of an emergency, especially in a remote location. Just remember that frequent ring-tones or talking loudly into a cellphone can be extremely irritating to others, so please use sparingly.

Something for your entertainment

Lounging around can get boring, even for the most indolent of us, so it's a good idea to take something to pass the time. Some reading matter, a portable CD or MP3 player (with earphones please), or some writing or painting materials will be useful.

First Aid Kit

Containing at a minimum:
Antiseptic cream.
A painkiller such as Paracetamol.

Antihistamine tablets.

Insect repellent.

Something for an upset stomach such as Imodium.

Alcohol-free cleansing wipes

Plasters/dressing.

Tweezers/scissors.

Always remember that you may be miles away from any shops, so be prepared!

Appendix 3

References, Links and Resources

In this section you will find a selection of links and other resources that will expand upon some of the ideas and information found in this book.

With so much information currently available on the internet, the challenge is not what to include but rather what to leave out. One could fill a book of this size with nudist links and still barely scratch the surface, and there are many sites on the internet that already do that particular job better than we can hope to here. These links and more can also be found on our own naturist blog, where they may be more easily updated, at *http://www.lovenaturism.com*.

Consequently we've limited ourselves to listing just those sites that will help you take the next steps on your nudist journey. Some of these sites contain their own comprehensive selection of nudist links, and as you explore further you'll find many more. We've also included links to sites that give more information about some of the points covered in the book, and we also list some suggested reading.

All the websites included have been chosen for their information and clarity and were active at the time of publication. To the best of our knowledge they are free of adult and unsuitable content, but sites, and the internet itself, evolve over time and all things change. *Use them at your own risk*. The inclusion of a site here does not guarantee that it will be accessible or free of adult material by the time you read this, nor does inclusion constitute an endorsement or recommendation.

For the sake of convenience we've used the excellent web redirection utilities *Snipurl* and *Bitly* to shorten some of the web addresses given in this book, as several of them were incredibly unwieldy.
Happy Hunting!

General Nudist Reference

Nudist Federations and Associations

International Naturist Federation/Federation Naturiste Internationale (INF/FNI)
http://www.inf-fni.org/
The home page of the INF / FNI, the umbrella organisation of the nudist Federations of over 30 countries and a good place to start. From here you can find the full contact details of your national federation. The website of your federation will list the individual clubs in your region.

American Association for Nude Recreation (AANR)
http://www.aanr.com/

British Naturism (BN)
http://www.bn.org.uk

Deutscher Verband für Freikörperkultur (DFK: Germany – otherwise known as FKK)
http://www.dfk.org/fkk/index.php/startseite

Naturisten Federatie Nederland (NFN: The Netherlands)
http://www.nfn.nl/

Australian Naturist Federation (ANF)
http://www.ausnatural.org.au

Fédération Francaise de Naturisme (FFN France)
http://www.ffn-naturisme.com

Nudist Beaches etc.

We've been unable to find a definitive listing of all naturist beaches worldwide, but the following sites are some of the best.

Nudist beaches

http://www.nudistbeaches.info/

Wikipedia's list of places where social nudity is practised.

http://bit.ly/1LNSL7d

This is a list of public outdoor clothes-free areas for recreation. It includes free beaches (or clothing-optional beaches or nude beaches), parks, clubs, regional organizations and some resorts.

Bare Beaches.com

http://www.barebeaches.com/

This is the website for the book '*The World's Best Nude Beaches and Resorts*' (ISBN: 9780954476731), which claims to give details of 1000 places to get naked. This is a well produced and excellently photographed book, although it covers more locations than most of us can ever hope to visit in one lifetime. You can purchase the book from the website.

Nudist Friendship, Dating and Community Sites

Singles Outdoor Club

http://www.soc-uk.info

A UK based naturist camping and walking club for single naturists.

Real Nudist Friends

http://realnudistfriends.com

A long established online nudist dating service especially for singles who enjoy nudist living, skinny dipping, meeting nudists, dating nudists and celebrating the nudist lifestyle.

Clothes-Free.com
http://www.clothesfree.com/
A web-based nudist club featuring a chat room, bulletin board, photos, news.

Nudist Holidays, Vacations and Travel

Castaways Travel
http://www.castawaystravel.com
A leading US based travel company specialising in clothing-optional and nude travel, resorts and cruises since 1984.

Bare Necessities Tour and Travel
https://www.cruisenude.com/
Another US company, Bare Necessities has been specialising in the finest clothing-optional vacations and nude cruises since 1990.

Away with Dune
http://www.awaywithdune.co.uk
The longest operating UK naturist tour operator offers worldwide vacations and cruises.

General Nudist Websites

Nudism on Wikipedia
http://en.wikipedia.org/wiki/Nudism
A good general introduction to nudism from this excellent on-line encyclopaedia with a good selection of links.

NudistExplorer.com
http://www.nudistexplorer.com/
A powerful search engine of thousands of nudist related pages with no adult sites.

Nudist Resorts. org
http://www.nudist-resorts.org/

Discussion forum for nudists and those interested in nude recreation, presented by the Society for Understanding Nudism.

Nudist UK
http://www.nudistuk.com/
A UK based website bringing you quality information and advice about nudism in the UK and beyond.

Clothes Free International
http://www.clothesfree.com/
Web-based nudist club with chat room, bulletin board, photos, news and more. US orientated.

The Naturist Society
http://www.naturist.com/
Membership of The Naturist Society offers an opportunity to learn more about the fascinating world of naturism.

Polls, surveys and chapter specific references

Chapter 1. An Overview

Roper Poll 2006
http://bit.ly/roperpoll
The 2006 Roper Poll into attitudes to nudism.

Chapter 2. History: Sources of information quoted in the text.

'humans started wearing garments only some 72,000 years ago.'
See 'Human body lice reveal the birthdate of fashion'
http://bit.ly/firstclothing

More about Pharaoh Akhenaten and his wife Nefertiti.
http://en.wikipedia.org/wiki/Akhenaten
http://en.wikipedia.org/wiki/Nefertiti

More about The Wandervogel
http://en.wikipedia.org/wiki/Wandervogel

Chapter 3. Twelve Reasons

'Those who wear bras even in bed are 125 TIMES more likely to get breast cancer than those who don't wear bras at all!'

See 'The health implications of wearing a bra.'

http://brafree.org

See also a general discussion of bra-wearing and health, and a history of the research into bras and breast disease. (From *The Spirit of Change* website)

http://bit.ly/1Ud7B7C

'Recent research has suggested an inverse relationship between solar exposure and cancer'

See 'Sunlight emerging as proven treatment for breast cancer, prostate cancer and other cancers.'

http://bit.ly/sunlightremedy

See also the scientific data

http://bit.ly/vitDrisk

'the benefits of regular sun exposure outweigh the risks of squamous-basal skin cancer'

See 'Beneficial effects of sun exposure on cancer mortality.'

http://bit.ly/ainsleigh

'fifty-five women die from underexposure to the sun to every one that dies of overexposure.'

See *http://bit.ly/betterbones1*

Body Image Problems

'33 per cent of men and an astonishing 75 per cent of women were dissatisfied with their physiques.'

See 'Differences In Body Image Between Men And Women.'

http://prevos.net/humanities/psychology/bodyimage/

Impartial, professional advice on penis enlargement from the UK's National Health Service

http://bit.ly/1Jj3IJk

Impartial, professional advice on weight loss from the UK's National Health Service.

http://bit.ly/1LAwnz7

Help on overcoming fear of nudity (Gymnophobia).

http://bit.ly/gymnophobia

Chapter 6. Christianity and nudism

Religious Tolerance

A site promoting religious freedom and diversity.

http://www.religioustolerance.org/nu_bibl.htm

Naturist Christians

A great site for anyone trying to reconcile Christianity with nudism.

http://www.naturist-christians.org/

The Gospel According to St Thomas

References to nudity (especially quote 37).

http://gnosis.org/naghamm/gthlamb.html

Chapter 9. Don't They Know That It's Different for Girls?

There is a huge amount of support and information available on the internet for lady nudists by lady nudists. Here is just a small selection to start with.

Cheri's Letter to a Reluctant Spouse

An open letter from a female nudist to a woman who is uncertain about her spouse's interest in nudism.

http://www.travelites.info/brochure.html

First Time Letter

Here's a letter from Vera, of the Diablo Sun Club in the USA, who tells us about her first time as a naturist.

http://bit.ly/first-time-letter

The Naturist Living Show: Women And Naturism
A YouTube presentation showing a selection of interviews with lady naturists, highlighting their problems, doubts and fears and how they overcame them. (Audio only.)
https://www.youtube.com/watch?v=txm1H2_2dNM

Chapter 11. Nudism and Children

Dr Benjamin Spock
http://en.wikipedia.org/wiki/Benjamin_Spock

Dr. Joyce Brothers
http://en.wikipedia.org/wiki/Joyce_Brothers

Dr. Lee Salk
https://en.wikipedia.org/wiki/Lee_Salk

Ted Polhemus
https://en.wikipedia.org/wiki/Ted_Polhemus
    See also:

Robin Lewis and Louis Janda 'The relationship between adult sexual adjustment and childhood experiences regarding exposure to nudity, sleeping in the parental bed, and parental attitudes toward sexuality.'
Lewis and Janda, (Archives of Sexual Behaviour, Vol 17/4, 1988)

Ron and Juliette Goldman 'Children's perceptions of clothes and nakedness: A cross-national study.'
Goldman and Goldman. Genetic Psychology Monographs 104 p163-185 (1981)

Marilyn Story 'Factors associated with more positive body self-concepts in preschool children.'
Story, Marilyn D, Journal of Social Psychology 108.1 (1979): 49-56

Casler, Lawrence. 'Some Sociopsychological Observations in a Nudist Camp: A Preliminary Study.'

Journal of Social Psychology 64 (1964): 307-323.

Chapter 12. Nudism and Health

Your local UV Index
http://www.uvawareness.com/

Miscellaneous Links

Information about Petanque
http://en.wikipedia.org/wiki/Petanque

The Burning Man Festival
http://en.wikipedia.org/wiki/Burning_man

World Naked Bike Ride
http://www.worldnakedbikeride.org/

World Body Painting Festival
http://www.bodypainting-festival.com/

World Naked Gardening Day
http://wngd.org/

Recommended Reading

Books either mentioned in the text or suggested for further reading.

Earthing Therapy: Nature's Most Powerful Natural Health Secret. (*Edgar*)
Ebook available from all good online booksellers. This little book looks into the science and practice of earth connection therapy or 'grounding', which helps you connect with the healing energies naturally present in the earth.

Dressed To Kill. (*Singer / Grismaier*) ISBN 978-1930858053
The authors have collected striking (but not universally accepted) evidence that bra-wearing may be a major risk factor associated with breast cancer.

Get It Off! (*Singer/ Grismaijer*) ISBN 978-1930858015
Get It Off begins where Dressed To Kill left off.

The World's Best Nude Beaches and Resorts (*Charles*)
ISBN 978-0934106221
This guide unveils the top 1,000 places where bare skin is simply the most fashionable thing to wear.

The Healing Sun (*Hobday*) ISBN 978-1899171972
This book explains how and why we should welcome sunlight back into our lives—safely! It shows how sunlight was used to prevent and cure diseases in the past, and how it can heal us and help us in the future.

Amongst The Nudists (*Merrill*) ISBN 978-1846641398
First published in 1931, this was the astonishing best-seller that brought nudism to the attention of millions of ordinary Americans for the first time and tempted them to try it for themselves.

The Naked Child Growing Up Without Shame (*Smith / Sparks*) ISBN 978-1555990015
Researchers Dennis Craig Smith and William Sparks spent over five years investigating the experiences of adults who had been brought up in an open physical environment.

Therapy, Nudity and Joy: Therapeutic Use of Nudity Through the Ages. (*Goodson*) ISBN 978-1555990282
The author interviewed nude patients, nudists and sex surrogates and claims that nudity works wonders for improving communication and eliminating sexual guilt and body shame.

Nudity: A Cultural Anatomy (*Barcan*) ISBN 978-1859738726
This book is a fascinating blend of meaningful minutiae and big philosophical questions about this most unnatural state of nature.

Nudity and Christianity (*Cunningham*) ISBN 978-1425975081
Jim Cunningham is an American Catholic 'freelance theologian' and in this book he explores all aspects of nudity and body consciousness in the context of Christian doctrine.

205 Arguments In Support Of Nudism (*Bacher*) (*http://snipurl.com/bacher2*)
This unique reference work, downloadable as an e-book free from our website in e-book form, will give you all the reasons you need to become a nudist.

About The Authors

James and Liz Egger are writers with an interest in personal development, natural therapies, eco-friendly living and, of course, nudism.

They have been keen naturists since the late 1970s. When they're not getting naked they enjoy listening to rock music, walking, travelling, and discovering and sampling delightful English country pubs.

You can meet and contact Liz at her author website at *http://www.lizegger.com/* or visit her own nudist website and blog at *http://www.lovenaturism.com*

If you'd like to take a look at her other naturist books just go to her Amazon author page (*amazon.com/author/lizegger* for the US or *http://www.amazon.co.uk/-/e/B00522WTNM* for the UK) where you'll find all her books conveniently displayed in one place, complete with covers, star rankings, pricing, reviews and an opportunity to sample each one.

For updates or information
This book will be revised and updated from time to time to keep it fresh, current and relevant, but in the meantime important revisions and updates can be found on our blog, or for quick reference, for readers of this book only, on the private page at *http://www.lovenaturism/updates/*.

Request for Reviews:

The authors invite you to share your opinions, thoughts and reactions to this book by writing a short review on Goodreads, your online bookseller's site, or on your favourite social media platforms.

Genuine feedback is immensely useful both to the authors and to other readers. Your support would be hugely appreciated.

More Books By Liz

Nice Girls Can Be Nudists Too

A collection of irreverent, entertaining and often very funny articles and essays on nudism and nakedness in which Liz takes a light-hearted and offbeat look at her life as a nudist and the absurdity of our attitude towards nudity and the naked body.

How to Get Naked and Not Get Arrested!

In this delightful book naturist Liz Egger takes a playful but informative look at the issue of nude leisure and the law. Whether you want to let it all hang out in your own back yard or whether your naked ambition extends to nudism and beyond, how can you be sure that you'll stay on the right side of the law? This book will help keep you on the straight and narrow, and even shows you how getting naked can earn you some useful extra cash.

Both books are e-books only, available in most digital formats at all good online booksellers.

Printed in April 2023
by Rotomail Italia S.p.A., Vignate (MI) - Italy